2005 Bankruptcy Revisions

Implications for Businesses and Financial Advisors

Edited by
Grant W. Newton
CPA, CIRA

Association of Insolvency and Restructuring Advisors
American Institute of Certified Public Accountants

Published jointly by

American Institute of Certified Public Accountants, Inc.
New York, New York 10036-8775

Association of Insolvency and Restructuring Advisors
Medford, Oregon 97501

ISBN 0-87051-618-3

About the Authors

Lawrence R. Ahern, III, Esq., Greenebaum Doll & McDonald PLLC, Nashville

Dennis Bean, CIRA, CPA, Dennis Bean & Company, Fresno

Vernon L. Calder, CIRA, CPA, Neilson Elggren LLP, Salt Lake City

James M. Lukenda, CIRA, CPA, Huron Consulting Group LLC, New York

Bob Pope, Esq., Gullett Sanford Robinson & Martin PLLC, Nashville

William H. Schrag, Esq., Morgan, Lewis & Bockius LLP, New York

Grant T. Stein, Esq., Alston & Bird LLP, Atlanta

Richard (Rob) Vanderbeek, CIRA, Huron Consulting Group, New York

Wendy S. Walker, Esq., Morgan, Lewis & Bockius LLP, New York

Jason H. Watson, Esq., Alston & Bird LLP, Atlanta

Jack F. Williams, CIRA, AIRA Scholar in Residence; Director, BDO Seidman; Professor, Georgia State University, Atlanta

About the Editor

Grant W. Newton, Professor of Accounting, Graziadio School of Business and Management, Pepperdine University, Malibu, California, is the Executive Director of the Association of Insolvency and Restructuring Advisors. He is a CPA and a CIRA, and received a Ph.D. from New York University. Dr. Newton was a member of the AICPA's Task Force on Financial Reporting by Entities in Reorganization Under the Bankruptcy Code, which resulted in the issuance of Statement of Position 90-7, *Financial Reporting by Entities in Reorganization Under the Bankruptcy Code*. He is the author of *Bankruptcy and Insolvency Accounting: Practice and Procedure* and *Bankruptcy and Insolvency Taxation*, both published by John Wiley & Sons (updated annually). He is coauthor of *Consulting Services Practice Aid 02-1: Business Valuation in Bankruptcy* and *Providing Bankruptcy & Reorganization Services—Practice Aid*, both published by the AICPA.

Table of Contents

Preface

The gauntlet is down; the trend is identified; the consequences are defined; the change is upon us.

All hyperbole and soothsaying aside, it is clear that the Bankruptcy Code as we have known it has changed. The amendments to the longstanding bankruptcy law are known as the Bankruptcy Abuse Prevention and Consumer Protection Act of 2005, and have created new responsibilities for practitioners who advise debtors as well as challenges to businesses that may become creditors or may themselves need to consider restructuring. The fundamental changes in the new law promise to change bankruptcy practice for generations.

In creating this reference book, the Certified Insolvency and Restructuring Advisors (CIRAs), CPAs, and attorneys devoted their time and shared their insights and expertise by participating in roundtable discussions on the ramifications of the new bankruptcy law and how it may affect current practice. Our hope is that the outcome of this work, by and for practitioners, will assist others in making sense of this complex new law.

It should be noted that Grant Newton spearheaded this entire project to bring you a concise, clearly written book focusing on the financial and tax aspects of the new Bankruptcy Act for businesses and consumers.

Each chapter of the book:

- Describes bankruptcy practices before the 2005 Act;
- Explains changes to the law; and
- Identifies specific practice areas that need to be closely examined.

Bankruptcy has never been a pleasant experience for anyone, but it is our hope that this book will serve as a ready reference for practitioners in their efforts to assist clients and businesses with negotiating the changes, nuances, and intricacies of the new law.

American Institute of Certified Public Accountants, Inc.
Association of Insolvency and Restructuring Advisors

Chapter 1

2005 Bankruptcy Act: Sweeping Changes

On April 20, 2005, President George W. Bush signed the Bankruptcy Abuse Prevention and Consumer Protection Act of 2005[1] (2005 Act). The 2005 Act represents in many ways the most significant change in the bankruptcy laws since the Bankruptcy Code (Code)[2] replaced the Bankruptcy Act in 1978. While the primary focus of the 2005 Act was on eliminating abuses of the law by consumers, there are provisions in the bill affecting almost all participants in the bankruptcy process—businesses, creditors, landlords, and the professionals involved in this field.

1.1 Purpose of the 2005 Act

Driven to a large extent by the credit card companies, there was a desire to make it harder for consumers to walk away from their debts. The motive underlying the 2005 Act is in its title, "Bankruptcy Abuse Prevention." Some of the underlying objectives driving the changes in the law were to:

- Use a means test as a method to reduce perceived abuses of the current system by requiring some individuals to either have their petition dismissed or agree to transfer to chapter 11 or 13 and make at least some debt payments with future income.
- Eliminate perceived abuses by consumers, in addition to limiting the extent to which individuals can walk away from their debts, by adjusting amounts available for homestead exemptions, for example, and increasing amounts that may be recovered from fraud.
- Reduce the time a business is in bankruptcy, as evidenced by, among other things, a limit on the time a debtor has to decide whether to assume or reject a lease and a limit on the amount of time a debtor has the exclusive right to develop a plan.
- Provide a source of tax revenue, especially for state and local governments, by changing the tax law to provide fewer tax benefits to individuals and businesses in bankruptcy. With a significant amount of influence from state attorneys general,

---

[1] Pub. L. No. 109–08, 119 Stat. 23.

[2] *Bankruptcy Code* and *Code* are used interchangeably throughout this publication.

the drafters of the law were convinced that state and local governments were at a disadvantage when it came to the collection of their taxes.

- Provide additional opportunities for creditors of businesses under certain conditions to recover all or a large percent of their prepetition claims by, for example, increasing the reclamation period and providing that goods shipped within 20 days of bankruptcy are administrative expenses.
- Reinstate chapter 12 on a permanent basis and make other changes perceived as necessary to the Bankruptcy Code.
- Provide protection to certain creditors, including, for example, those owed amounts for domestic support obligations and secured creditors in chapter 13.

1.2 2005 Act Content

The 2005 Act consists of over 500 pages and 16 different titles. This publication focuses on the following four major topics spread throughout a large number of the Act's titles:

- Business changes, including cross-border issues
- Tax changes
- Means testing
- Consumer abuses and protection

All these provisions are discussed in detail in the chapters that follow. Chapters 2 through 10 deal with changes in the bill affecting businesses; Chapters 11 and 12 focus primarily on consumer issues. Chapter 11 deals with the already controversial means test, and Chapter 12 deals with several other consumer issues, including the homestead exemption. Chapters 13 through 15 analyze some of the key tax issues, and Chapter 16 provides a summary of the impacts this legislation is expected to have on bankruptcy practice.

1.3 Issues Needing Resolution

While many provisions of the 2005 Act were proposed over eight years ago, there was limited opportunity for input on the various bills considered. As a result, the 2005 Act contains conflicts and unresolved issues that have only begun to be addressed.

Such conflicts and issues needing resolution are obvious in the tax law changes. For example, the 2005 Act changes the interest rate on tax claims from a market rate to the rate of interest that would be used in nonbankruptcy situations. While the rate for federal taxes approximates market value, the rate for state and local taxes could be in excess of 20 percent, resulting in state and local taxing authorities receiving interest in excess of the market rate at the expense of other creditors. This change violates the general philosophy underlying bankruptcy law that creditors should not receive consideration in excess of the value of their claims. Yet this change has been made with limited opportunity to discuss the impact it might have.

Another example of a significant issue to be resolved lies in the stipulation that income earned by a chapter 11 debtor subsequent to petition filing will, under the 2005 Act, become part of the bankruptcy estate. For individuals, a separate taxable estate is created in chapter 11, but not in chapter 13. However, according to tax law, individual debtors in chapter 13 will continue to file individual returns with no separate estate created and report all income and expenses as if no petition were filed. Conversely, under chapter 11 a separate estate *is* created for tax purposes; the estate files a separate income tax return; income earned after petition filing is treated as income of the individual; and individual tax returns are submitted for activity by the individual debtor after petition filing. However, the 2005 Act provides that in chapter 11, all income earned by the individual is now property of the estate. No changes have been made in the tax laws to deal with the inconsistencies that have been created.

1.4 Bankruptcy Rules and Forms

Because insufficient time was provided before the date of enactment for the promulgation of rules under the Rules Enabling Act, courts are urged to adopt the Interim Bankruptcy Rules, which were approved by the Advisory Committee on Bankruptcy Rules and the Committee on Rules of Practice and Procedure.

The Interim Rules and Forms are expected to apply to bankruptcy cases from October 17, 2005, until final rules and forms are promulgated and effective under the regular Rules Enabling Act process. In August 2006, the Advisory Committee and Committee on Rules of Practice and Procedure expect to publish for public comment a proposed new and amended Federal Rules of Bankruptcy Procedure—based substantially on the Interim Rules modified as appropriate after consideration of comments from the bench and bar as a result of the use of the Interim Rules—along with any additional revisions to the Official Forms. In the meantime, the Advisory Committee will review the experiences of the bench, bar, and public and seeks written comments on the use of the Interim Rules and Official Forms. Comments may be sent to: Peter G. McCabe, Secretary, Committee on Rules of Practice and Procedure, Thurgood Marshall Federal Judiciary Building, Washington, D.C. 20544.

1.5 Effective Dates

The Act generally applies to all cases filed on or after October 17, 2005; however, several provisions were made effective for cases commenced on or after April 20, 2005 (the date of enactment). A few of the provisions were even made specifically applicable to cases pending as of the enactment date. Information about effective dates for the provisions covered in this publication is included at the end of the chapter or section that discusses the provisions.

1.6 Purpose of This Publication

The purpose of this publication is to identify, explain, and discuss probable significant effects of the major provisions included in the 2005 Bankruptcy Act applicable to businesses and financial advisors. The majority of the chapters follow the process of briefly describing the practice prior to the 2005 Act, explaining the provisions of the 2005 Act, and then discussing some of its potential impacts.

1.7 Proposed Relief to Hurricane Katrina's Victims

This publication is being sent to the printer 10 days after the terrible disaster caused by Hurricane Katrina. There is considerable discussion at this time about granting special relief to Katrina's victims. Two major proposals are under consideration: The first is to modify the current bankruptcy law to specifically exclude the hurricane victims from the means testing provision (see Chapter 11) of the 2005 Act scheduled to go into effect for all petitions filed on or after October 17, 2005. The second option is to delay the effective date of the 2005 Act for one to two years or longer. The proponents of the 2005 Act note that the new law already gives the Bankruptcy Court the right to waive provisions under special circumstances, for example, "an act of God." It would be expected that bankruptcy judges in the areas devastated by Katrina would be sympathetic to the cases of these victims, many of whom have incomes below the median income standard as a result of the loss of jobs.

Special challenges will be faced by individuals with income levels below the median, who will have difficulty locating tax returns and other information to support their appeal for relief under the special circumstance provision of the Code and to preclude abuse provisions from applying. In addition, according to the 2005 Act, these individuals will be required to undergo financial counseling when their need to file is caused by an act of God and not their own financial mismanagement. As those implementing the major consumer changes in the 2005 Act begin their task, there will be a major increase in filings due to the damage caused by Katrina, creating additional problems of delays and red-tape snarls for the victims of Katrina.

To obtain additional information about any delays or changes to the 2005 Act due to Hurricane Katrina, please visit http://www.airacira.org/ bankruptcy_law_changes.

Chapter 2

Leases and Executory Contracts

2.1 Introduction

Some of the most significant provisions among the commercial changes of the Bankruptcy Abuse Prevention and Consumer Protection Act of 2005 (2005 Act) affect parties to executory contracts and unexpired leases. The balance of power between landlords and tenants and between parties to executory contracts is often critical to the outcome of a reorganization. That balance of power has been changed by the 2005 Act in several ways, some dramatic and others more subtle. This chapter focuses first on the rules that apply particularly to the relationship between commercial debtors and their landlords. Then, it will look at the broader impact of the amendments on landlords and tenants, lessors and lessees of personal property, and parties to executory contracts in general.

2.2 Special Rules for Nonresidential Real Estate Leases (2005 Act Section 404)

(a) Practice Prior to 2005 Act

Insolvency advisors who have worked with real estate developers and others owning commercial space have long complained of their clients' frustration as landlords with respect to the length of time for assumption or rejection of leases in chapter 11. The interests of lessors are affected by the fact that, by nature, reorganization in bankruptcy is partly designed to give debtors adequate time to reorganize. For example, reorganizing retailers have been allowed to wait through a business cycle before assuming all of their obligations to landlords. Although the Bankruptcy Code prior to amendment already required that leases be assumed or rejected within 60 days after filing, the courts were allowed to extend this deadline and often did so. [Former 11 U.S.C. §365(d) (applying the 60-day standard with varying degrees of severity in cases under all chapters of the Code)]

Note: Lawrence R. Ahern III is co-author of the Thomson/West publication, *2005 Bankruptcy Reform Legislation with Analysis*, part of which formed the basis for this chapter and is printed here with permission. Thanks to David W. Houston IV for his contribution to this chapter and to Mr. Houston and Darlene T. Marsh for their review of the manuscript.

These extensions often lasted for many months and, especially in large cases, sometimes delayed landlords' ability to exercise their rights for years. The 2005 Act tilts the playing field considerably in the landlords' direction. Whereas landlords may believe the effect is simply to level the field, other creditors may be less happy with the outcome.

(b) New Deadlines to Assume or Reject

The 2005 Act section 404 amended former Code section 365(d)(4) to provide that unexpired leases of nonresidential real estate in which the debtor is the lessee are deemed rejected and must be immediately surrendered to the lessor by the earlier of 120 days after the commencement of the case or the date of the confirmation of a plan. The court, for cause, may extend the 120 day period for an additional 90 days, but any extension subsequent to the additional 90 days is available only with the consent of the lessor.

(c) Impact of Change

The new law thus provides for *automatic* rejection of a nonresidential real estate lease, if the reorganizing tenant does not assume the lease, and it imposes a strict timeline on the process. [11 U.S.C. §365(d)(4)] At the end of the specified schedule of events, the landlord is given a veto over the tenant's ability to extend the deadline further. This new timeline is designed to focus judges' attention on the interests of landlords and, over the course of the bankruptcy process, to increase pressure on the tenant. Large retail companies and other companies with a significant number of nonresidential real property leases will find it necessary to complete extensive lease analyses prior to petition filing. Additionally, the timing of filing will be affected because retail entities will avoid filing petitions during the seven- eight-, or even nine-month period prior to peak season, if at all possible.

(d) Rejection Timeline

The new schedule for rejection or assumption works this way: In a voluntary chapter 11 filed on or after October 17, 2005, the timeline starts with the filing of the petition itself. [*Id.* (measuring the deadline is from the order for relief)]

First 120 Days

From this starting point (the date of the order for relief), the tenant has 120 days within which to make a decision about the wisdom of assuming the lease. The first 120 days of the case allows the debtor a period in which to assess its situation; however, the deadline may be reduced by request. If in the meantime the tenant proposes a plan of reorganization (files a plan with the bankruptcy court), the 120 days is cut short at the date the court confirms the plan of reorganization. In other words, there is automatic rejection if the lease is not assumed by the earlier of (1) 120 days after the commencement of the voluntary case or (2) the entry of a confirmation order.

90 More Days

After the initial four-month grace period, the court may only extend the deadline (1) for cause and (2) for a time not to exceed 90 days. To be granted the additional 90-day extension after the first four months (or 120 days), the debtor is required to show "cause" for the extension; perhaps because it must wait to see whether its business prospects improve. Added together, the 120 days plus 90 more days gives the reorganizing tenant a maximum grace period of seven months within which to assume the lease or face automatic rejection. One final possibility for further extension exists under certain conditions, as described below.

Further Extensions

After the 210 days (or 7 months) of the two initial extensions, further delay of the assumption/rejection process may be allowed *only with "the prior written consent of the lessor,"* who may thus stop the process. It may well be that granting additional time makes sense, but at that point it is the landlord's prerogative to make the decision.

(e) Postassumption, Postrejection Lease Claims

These rules may have some unpleasant (and perhaps unintended) consequences. Under the former law, an assumed lease became an obligation of the bankruptcy estate, just as if the trustee or debtor-in-possession had entered into a new lease. If the estate rejected or otherwise defaulted under this contract, the result was a priority administrative claim for the unpaid rent. Thus, trade creditors (and even other landlords, whose leases are *not* assumed) may now find themselves distressed by the result of the 2005 Act's pressure on the estate, because landlords who are able to force the assumption of their leases might put themselves in a priority position that may eviscerate the value of the estate in an ultimate liquidation. These side effects of the new law should not be ignored as trade creditors and landlords consider the dynamics of dealing with a tenant under the new chapter 11 regime.

The 2005 Act does, however, attempt to deal with the reality that debtors may be forced into premature assumption of leases that are ultimately defaulted. In an apparent effort by Congress to ameliorate the effect on unsecured creditors that would be caused by such premature assumption followed by later rejection, the amended Code limits the administrative claim resulting from that circumstance. Landlords are allowed to have a priority claim of up to two years' rent and other monetary damages after the ultimate rejection or turnover of the leased property, whichever occurs later. [11 U.S.C. §503(b)(7)] For a more detailed discussion of this and other priority claims, see Chapter 9 of this publication. The balance of landlords' claims would be relegated to unsecured status, subject to the cap imposed by Code section 502(b)(6).

2.3 Rules Related to All Unexpired Leases and Executory Contracts (2005 Act Sections 309 and 328)

(a) Cure of Nonmonetary Defaults

One of the recent and more contentious battles between landlords, tenants and other parties to executory contracts has been fought over the need to cure defaults in the assumption process. Before the 2005 Act, paragraph (1) of former Code section 365(b) required a debtor-in-possession or a trustee, if appointed, that is assuming the lease or executory contract to cure or provide for the cure of defaults before assumption, but subsection (b) went on to provide:

> (2) paragraph (1) of this subsection does not apply to a default that is a breach of a provision relating to—
>
> . . .
>
> (D) the satisfaction of any penalty rate or provision relating to a default arising from any failure by the debtor to perform non-monetary obligations under the executory contract or unexpired lease.

[*Former Code section 365(b)(2)(D)*]

The interpretation of this language produced a split in the decisions of the federal circuit courts, which Congress has now attempted to resolve.

The circuit split is found in *In re Claremont Acquisition Corporation, Inc.,* [113 F.3d 1029 (9th Cir. 1997)] and *In re Bankvest Capital Corp.* [360 F.3d 291 (1st Cir. 2004)]. In *Bankvest* and *Claremont*, the two circuits analyzed former Code section 365(b)(2)(D) and came to different conclusions as to whether the language required that debtors cure nonmonetary defaults prior to assuming executory contracts and unexpired leases.

The *Claremont* case arose from the attempted assumption of a franchise agreement for a car dealership. Prior to the debtor's bankruptcy, the debtor had ceased operations for a period of 14 days. The franchise agreement required that the operations at the dealership be continuous, and, thus, the shutdown breached the franchise agreement. When the debtor attempted to assume the franchise agreement, the franchisor objected and argued that the debtor's failure to abide by the continuous operation requirement constituted an "historical" default which the debtor could not cure. [*See In re Claremont*, 113 F.3d at 1033] The debtor argued that the continuous operation requirement is a nonmonetary obligation, and under former Code section 365(b)(2)(D), the debtor is not required to cure nonmonetary defaults. [*Id.*]

Siding with the franchisor, the *Claremont* court determined that former Code section 365(b)(2)(D) *only* exempted from the debtor's cure requirements the *payment of monetary penalties* resulting from the failure to perform nonmonetary obligations. [*Id.* at 1034.] Thus, the Ninth Circuit read the word *penalty* (meaning penalty payment) in former paragraph (2)(D) to modify both nouns following that modifier, *rate* and *provision*, determining this to be the only proper grammatical reading of the former language. So, if either a penalty rate or other penalty payment was tied to a nonmonetary obligation, it need not be cured, but other nonmonetary defaults had to be cured, regardless of whether it was possible to do so. The court's decision was based in part on its review of the limited legislative history of the former Code section, which suggested that debtors will be able to assume a lease by curing any default at the nondefault interest rate. The *Claremont* court took this to mean that Congress only intended to protect debtors from being required to pay monetary penalties resulting from nonmonetary defaults. The Ninth Circuit reasoned that the debtor's proposed reading of former Code section 365(b)(2)(D) would render the other three subsections useless or superfluous in that they would be covered by subsection (D). [*Id.*] Thus, all nonmonetary defaults were to be cured unless such default requires a payment by the debtor of a monetary penalty.

In *Bankvest*, the First Circuit took the opposite approach. The court observed that the *Claremont* ruling produced a harsh result for debtors by creating situations in which the debtor's ability to cure a default under an expired lease or executory contract would be impossible. [See *In re Bankvest*, 360 F.3d at 299.] The *Bankvest* Court found the result reached in *Claremont* to be at odds with the underlying principles of the Bankruptcy Code, namely the rehabilitation of debtors. [*Id.* at 300]. The First Circuit concluded that debtors may assume executory contracts and unexpired leases without first curing *any* nonmonetary defaults.

(b) Changes Enacted

In the 2005 Act, Congress has addressed this split in the circuits by taking pages from both the *Claremont* and *Bankvest* opinions. First, in construing the language of former Code section 365(b)(2)(D), Congress sided with the *Claremont* court. Subsection (b)(2)(D) now reads as follows:

> (2) Paragraph (1) of this subsection does not apply to a default that is a breach of a provision relating to—
>
> . . .
>
> (D) The satisfaction of any penalty rate or *penalty* provision relating to a default arising from any failure by the debtor to perform non-monetary obligations under the executory contract or unexpired lease.

[*11 U.S.C. §365(b)(2)(D) (new text in italics)*]

This change results in the same phrasing inferred by the *Claremont* court with the word *penalty* modifying both nouns, *rate* and *provision*. Congress therefore has agreed with the view that Code section 365(b)(2)(D) should only except from debtors' cure obligations the payment of penalty rates or penalty provisions but that the escape clause (b)(2)(D) does not provide a catch-all exception for nonmonetary defaults. Unless the nonmonetary default requires some type of penalty payment, the debtor must cure the nonmonetary default prior to assumption.

However, Congress attempted to reduce somewhat the harsh effects illuminated in *Bankvest*, particularly for commercial landlords, by adding the following language to Code section 365(b)(1)(A):

> (b)(1) if there has been a default in an executory contract or unexpired lease of the debtor, the trustee may not assume such contract or lease unless, at the time of assumption of such contract or lease, the trustee—
>
> > (A) cures, or provides adequate assurance that the trustee will promptly cure, such default *other than a default that is a breach of a provision relating to the satisfaction of any provision (other than a penalty rate or penalty provision) relating to a default arising from any failure to perform nonmonetary obligations under any unexpired lease of real property, if it is impossible for the trustee to cure such default by performing non-monetary acts at and after the time of assumption, except that if such default arises from a failure to operate in ac-*

> *cordance with a non-residential real property lease, then such default shall be cured by performance at and after the time of assumption in accordance with such lease, and pecuniary losses resulting from such default shall be compensated in accordance with the provisions of this paragraph;*

[*11 U.S.C. §365(b)(1)(A) (new text in italics)*]

The additional language of the 2005 Act specifically exempts certain nonmonetary cure obligations of the debtor. These exceptions, however, only apply to unexpired leases of real property. Thus, the result reached in *Claremont* would be the same today under section 365(b)(1) and (2) because *Claremont* dealt with a franchise agreement and not a real property lease.

Note that the 2005 changes do not except from the debtor's cure requirements every nonmonetary obligation under leases of real property. This is true in two respects. First, the 2005 Act only excepts those nonmonetary acts that are "impossible" for the debtor to cure at or after the time of assumption. A new debate will certainly arise over what cure obligations are impossible.

Furthermore, the language under new paragraph 365(b)(1)(A) specifically requires that, at and after the time of assumption, the debtor perform any breach related to the failure to operate in accordance with a nonresidential real property lease. Debtors are therefore compelled to comply prospectively with all operational terms in nonresidential real property leases. The distinction between "operating" and nonoperating obligations may also be a source of debate.

(c) Impact of Changes

Congress' modifications to former Code section 365 should add some clarity to the proper interpretation of Code section 365(b)(2)(D). In the case of real property leases, the new language will prevent the harsh result articulated in *Bankvest*. However, in all other situations including franchise agreements, leases of personal property, and any other executory contracts or unexpired leases that are not leases of real property, the existence of a nonmonetary default that triggers a nonmonetary obligation of the debtor seems to provide the nondebtor party a means to block the assumption of otherwise valuable contracts. In many situations, these counterparties will thus continue to hold a trump card that may affect the debtor's ability to successfully reorganize. This is true because the *Claremont* rule continues to apply for all executory contracts and unexpired leases except "impossible" cure obligations in residential real estate leases and impossible cure of any obligations in nonresidential real estate leases.

The outcome of the particular facts in *Claremont* apparently would be the same under the 2005 Act, while the *Bankvest* decision would be reversed, as illustrated by the following matrix of facts and results.

Analysis of Possible Circumstances and Outcomes Under Amended Section 365

- Personal Property Lease
  - Monetary default: Cure required
  - Nonmonetary default with payment penalty: Cure not required
  - Nonmonetary default with no payment penalty: Cure required (Note: These are the *Bankvest* facts and cure would be required.)
- Executory Contract (for example, Franchise Agreement)
  - Monetary default: Cure required
  - Nonmonetary default with payment penalty: Cure not required
  - Nonmonetary default with no payment penalty: Cure required (Note: These are the *Claremont* facts and cure would still be required.)
- Nonresidential Real Estate Lease
  - Monetary default: Cure required
  - Nonmonetary default with payment penalty: Cure not required
  - Nonmonetary default with no payment penalty: Cure not required if "impossible" except cure for failure to operate in accordance with the lease prospectively
- Residential Real Estate Lease
  - Monetary default: Cure required
  - Nonmonetary default with payment penalty: Cure not required
  - Nonmonetary default with no payment penalty: Cure not required if "impossible"

Note: It continues to be necessary to provide compensation to the lessor or counterparty for pecuniary losses resulting from any such default.

(d) Personal Property Leases

Two final notes: A chapter 7 debtor is now specifically permitted to assume an unexpired lease of personal property. [11 U.S.C. §365(p)(2)] In chapter 11 or 13 cases, however, if an individual debtor does not assume the lease in a plan, the lease would be rejected and not subject to the automatic stay. [11 U.S.C. §365(p)(3)]

2.4 Effective Date of Changes

The provisions of the 2005 Bankruptcy Reform Act generally are effective for cases filed on or after October 17, 2005. All of the provisions discussed in this chapter become effective for cases filed on or after October 17, 2005.

Chapter 3

Employee Compensation and Conflicts

3.1 Key Employee Retention and Severance Programs (2005 Act Section 331)

The retention of key management personnel is a critical area that has regularly attracted controversy among parties in chapter 11 reorganizations. With the advent of a chapter 11 filing, incentive compensation opportunities for management such as stock-based compensation must be reexamined. Over time, specific programs to deal with compensation-related management issues have evolved and become a regular part of the chapter 11 process. These programs generally deal with three broad compensation areas: incentive compensation, severance, and retention.

Incentive compensation plans adopted in conjunction with a chapter 11 filing generally seek to replace lost incentive benefits that are tied to options or stock that may have become worthless as a result of the company's financial difficulties. They may also be necessary to reset financial targets in light of the chapter 11 filing. Typically, chapter 11 incentive compensation plans are cash plans that link management's performance to company objectives related to the company's turnaround and emergence from chapter 11.

Postpetition severance programs are designed to provide employees with income security for a period that should approximate the time it might take the employee to find new employment in case the company concludes that a covered employee's service is no longer necessary to the reorganization process.

Generally more controversial than either incentive or severance programs, Key Employee Retention Programs (KERPs) have the stated objective of providing monetary incentives to targeted employees to induce them to remain with the company for a defined period. Generally directed at top management, KERPs have come under constant fire from creditors and other parties.

(a) Practice Prior to 2005 Act

Under Code section 105(a), debtors sought approval of KERP payments from the bankruptcy court based upon the common-law "necessity doctrine," which grants administrative expense status on "necessary costs and expenses of preserving the estate" related to wages, salaries and commissions for postpetition services.

KERP payments have also been approved under Code section 363(b), which provides that "the trustee, after notice and a hearing, may use, sell or lease, other than in the ordinary course of business, property of the estate."

Bankruptcy courts have found the debtor's use of reasonable retention bonuses and other incentives to retain key employees is a valid exercise of the debtor's business judgment.

(b) Changes Enacted

Under new Code section 503(c), effective October 17, 2005, a debtor is prohibited from paying any amount to an insider for the purpose of inducing that person to remain with the company unless specific requirements are met:

- The person must have a "bona fide job offer" from another or similar business at the "same or greater rate of compensation."
- The services of the person must be "essential to the survival of the business."
- The amount of a transfer or obligation to an insider cannot exceed 10 times the mean of similar payments made to non-management employees during the calendar year in which the transfer is made.
- If no such payments were made, the limit is 25 percent of any similar payments made to the insider for any purpose during the prior calendar year.

The text for new section 503(c) follows:

> *(c) Notwithstanding subsection (b), there shall neither be allowed, nor paid—*
>
> > *(1) a transfer made to, or an obligation incurred for the benefit of, an insider of the debtor for the purpose of inducing such person to remain with the debtor's business, absent a finding by the court based on evidence in the record that—*
> >
> > > *(A) the transfer or obligation is essential to retention of the person because the individual has a bona fide job offer from another business at the same or greater rate of compensation;*
> > >
> > > *(B) the services provided by the person are essential to the survival of the business; and*
> > >
> > > *(C) either—*
> > >
> > > > *(i) the amount of the transfer made to, or obligation incurred for the benefit of, the*

person is not greater than an amount equal to 10 times the amount of the mean transfer or obligation of a similar kind given to nonmanagement employees for any purpose during the calendar year in which the transfer is made or the obligation is incurred; or

(ii) if no such similar transfers were made to, or obligations were incurred for the benefit of, such nonmanagement employees during such calendar year, the amount of the transfer or obligation is not greater than an amount equal to 25 percent of the amount of any similar transfer or obligation made to or incurred for the benefit of such insider for any purpose during the calendar year before the year in which such transfer is made or obligation is incurred;

(2) a severance payment to an insider of the debtor, unless—

(A) the payment is part of a program that is generally applicable to all full-time employees; and

(B) the amount of the payment is not greater than 10 times the amount of the mean severance pay given to nonmanagement employees during the calendar year in which the payment is made; or

[*11 U.S.C. §503(c)(1) and (2)) (new text in italics)*]

Insiders may not receive a severance payment unless the payment is part of a program generally applicable to all full-time employees and the amount is not greater than 10 times the amount of the mean severance payment made to nonmanagement employees.

(c) Impact of Changes

The new law places significant limitations on retention and severance payments. Congress's intention was to curb a perceived problem with rewarding management while the rank and file suffered. The impact of this change could create difficulties in retaining executives who have the special skills or institutional knowledge that can be critical to successful reorganization.

Although amendments to this section of the Code illustrate Congress's aim to prevent the abuse of compensation incentives for insiders, the new laws make chapter 11 a less attractive alternative to the management of a troubled company.

One purpose of a KERP is to compensate executives for foregoing the opportunity to look for other employment in the market place. As enacted, the Bankruptcy Abuse Prevention and Consumer Protection Act of 2005 (2005 Act) amendments create an unworkable situation requiring executives to seek other employment offers, in order to justify compensation for the risk of not pursuing those alternatives, at a time when the executive's full attention should be given over to the company's problems. The practical impact of the amendment will be to divert the attention of executives by forcing them to initiate the job search process that a KERP is designed to forestall.

Another consequence of the 2005 Act is that the formulas included in the legislation could result in reduction or elimination of retention payments to nonmanagement employees. Executives may not want to make any retention payments to nonmanagement employees in order to eliminate a potential cap on transfers granted to them for retention. Assuming no payments are made to nonmanagement employees, even at 25 percent of similar payments, potential KERP payments will be well below existing market levels.

As a result of the new legislation, alternative such as wider use of performance incentive plans may develop. Management will not be compensated for staying but rather for achieving defined objectives and milestones in corporate performance and restructuring.

For financial advisors, the impact of the new legislation will include more planning to evaluate the imposed limitations (for example, calculation of mean retention and severance payments within defined timeframes) and assistance with the development and evaluation of performance-based incentive programs.

3.2 Postpetition Hires (2005 Act Section 331)

New Code section 503(c)(3) adds a prohibition against payments that are outside of the ordinary course of business and not justified by the "facts and circumstances" of the case:

> *(3) other transfers or obligations that are outside the ordinary course of business and not justified by the facts and circumstances of the case, including transfers made to, or obligations incurred for the benefit of, officers, managers, or consultants hired after the date of the filing of the petition.*

[*11 U.S.C. §365(c)(3) (new text in italics)*]

Professionals who are hired after the petition is filed need to be sure that if their tasks are outside or appear to be outside of the ordinary course of business, the court in approving their employment rules that such employment is appropriately justified. This provision is intended to apply to an incentive-based compensation package for a new executive or to retain a consultant, but it could be interpreted more broadly.

Incentive payments to employees or consultants hired postpetition may not change significantly under this provision, since courts typically require such findings already. However, compensation to chief restructuring officers (CROs), turnaround professionals, or other consultants could be subject to this provision. Thus, it becomes even more important for the court to rule that such employment is justified based on the needs of the service and other factors, such as the lack of experienced personnel inside the troubled business.

3.3 Fraudulent Transfers (2005 Act Section 1402)

The amendments to Code section 548, Fraudulent Transfers and Obligations, provide new tools to reach back and reclaim previously paid compensation. See 8.3 for additional discussion of the changes in the fraudulent transfer provisions.

The "look-back" period for fraudulent transfers and obligations is increased to two years and specifically provides for the avoidance of a transfer to an insider under an employment contract. Thus, under Code section 548, action may be taken to recover an amount involved in a fraudulent transfer, provided the transfer occurs within two years prior to the filing of the petition. Action may still be taken in the bankruptcy court if the transfer occurred more than two years prior to filing, but only under state statues and not under Code section 548. New Code section 548(a)(1)(B)(ii)(IV) adds a provision that would permit avoidance of out of the ordinary course employment contracts of insiders without proof of insolvency as follows:

> *(IV) made such transfer to or for the benefit of an insider, or incurred such obligation to or for the benefit of an insider, under an employment contract and not in the ordinary course of business.*

[*11 U.S.C. §548(a)(1)(B)(ii)(IV) (new text in italics)*]

The provision covering employment contracts is effective immediately, while the extension of the look-back period from one year to two years will be effective one year after enactment. As with new Code section 503(C)(3), prepetition compensation to CROs, turnaround professionals, and other consultants could be subject to this provision as well.

3.4 Priority Claims for Employee Benefits (2005 Act Section 1401)

(a) Practice Prior to 2005 Act

Among the first-day motions typically presented to the court are requests for orders related to the continuation of employee pay, benefits, and benefit programs. Not only are these motions justified by the critical nature of a workforce to a debtor's survival, but also as an extension of the priority allowed to such benefits under Code section 507, Priorities. Under Code section 507(a)(3), individuals and corporations had a third priority for unpaid wages and other benefits earned within 90 days before the date of the filing to the extent of $4,925 per individual or corporation.

(b) Changes Enacted

Effective for petitions filed on or after April 20, 2005, Code section 507 is amended to broaden the priority protection for certain employee claims.

- The look-back period for priority wage and benefit plan claims will be increased from 90 to 180 days.
- The cap for wage and benefit plan claims will be raised from $4,925 to $10,000.

In addition, the formula for determining the cap for priority status of contributions to an employee benefit plan is amended to incorporate the increase in the cap in the wage and benefit plan claims from the current $4,925 to $10,000.

(c) Impact of Changes

These changes in Code section 507 could result in an increase in cash needs after the bankruptcy filing. Following the existing practice of first-day motions requesting authority for debtors to pay out amounts to employees up to the established priority, additional funds may be necessary since the cap is being doubled.

In all likelihood, employee benefit plans will also benefit to the detriment of general unsecured creditors at plan time. After considering the individual employee claims, the cap increase could provide for greater priority claims for employee benefit plans, leaving less value available for general unsecured creditors.

3.5 Retiree Benefits (2005 Act Section 1403)

A new Code section 1114(l) is added:

> *(l) If the debtor, during the 180-day period ending on the date of the filing of the petition—*
>
> > *(1) modified retiree benefits; and*
> >
> > *(2) was insolvent on the date such benefits were modified; the court, on motion of a party in interest, and after notice and a hearing, shall issue an order reinstating as of the date the modification was made, such benefits as in effect immediately before such date unless the court finds that the balance of the equities clearly favors such modification.*

[*11 U.S.C. §1114(l) (new text in italics)*]

Under this section, if a debtor has modified retiree benefits during the 180-day period before the chapter 11 filing and was insolvent at the time, the court may reinstate the benefits as of the date of modification unless the court finds that the balance of the equities clearly favors the modification. This section is effective for bankruptcy cases filed on or after April 20, 2005, the date of enactment of the 2005 Act.

Bankruptcy planning will require a closer examination of the effect and timing of modifications to retiree benefits as a result of this change. It is unclear at this point whether contractual modifications (for example, an increase in retiree medical co-payments corresponding to an increase in co-payments of active employees) would be subject to Code section 1114(l). In the event that benefits are reinstated, not only would prepetition claims be increased, but significant additional administrative expense could be added to a debtor's business plan. A debtor and its financial advisors should have detailed analyses supporting the economic and business case for any changes in retiree benefits and should have analyses of the potential impact a reinstatement could have on the postpetition operating and cash flow plan.

3.6 Wages and Benefits Awarded as Back Pay (2005 Act Section 329)

(a) Practice Prior to 2005 Act

Under the previous law, awards pursuant to a judicial proceeding after the commencement of a bankruptcy case were prepetition claims against the debtor if the wrongful conduct giving rise to the award occurred before the bankruptcy petition was filed.

(b) Changes Enacted

The 2005 Act amends Code section 503(b)(1)(A) to require administrative expense status for the portion of wages and benefits awarded pursuant to a judicial or National Labor Relations Board proceeding as back pay attributable to any period of time after the bankruptcy filing. This amendment is effective immediately for cases filed on or after April 20, 2005.

As provided in the amendment, the administrative expense status of the portion of the award related to postpetition back wages is contingent upon a determination of the court that the payment of the wages and benefits will not substantially increase the probability of a layoff or termination of current employees, or of nonpayment of domestic support obligations during the bankruptcy case.

(c) Impact of Changes

For debtors defending labor-related class action suits or with recurring labor problems, this amendment could have significant impact on postpetition cash flow and on the debtor's ability to confirm a plan of reorganization. Among other issues a debtor must consider is the analysis of the probability that payment of individual or serial awards will result in the layoff or termination of current employees.

3.7 Retention of Financial Professionals (2005 Act Section 414)

(a) Practice Prior to 2005 Act

To be retained as a professional in a bankruptcy case, Code section 327(a) required, among other things, that the professional be a "disinterested person." This requirement of "disinterestedness" has limited the ability of certain investment bankers and attorneys to be retained in bankruptcy cases.

As previously defined, a disinterested person is one who, among other things, is not or has not been within three years before the bankruptcy filing, an investment banker for any outstanding security of the debtor or an attorney for an investment banker in connection with the offer, sale, or issuance of a security of the debtor.

(b) Changes Enacted

Section 101(14) has been amended to remove the language that excluded an investment banker or an attorney for an investment banker for any outstanding security of the debtor from the definition of "disinterested person."

(c) Impact of Changes

Although an investment banker or attorney for an investment banker involved in securities of the debtor will be eligible to be retained, the investment banker must still not have a materially adverse interest to the estate or to any class of creditors or equity security holders. Many bankruptcy cases have accompanying securities litigation. In light of this, the "no materially adverse interest" requirement may not be easy to meet for investment banking firms that handled the debtor's securities offerings prior to the bankruptcy filing.

3.8 Compensation Arrangements (2005 Act Section 1206)

Code section 328(a) provided that bankruptcy professionals may be retained under reasonable terms and conditions including retention on an hourly or contingent fee basis. Although long accepted as a means of compensation in many courts, fixed or percentage fee bases were not specifically provided for. Section 328(a) provides:

> **§328. Limitation on compensation of professional persons**
>
> (a) The trustee, or a committee appointed under section 1102 of this title, with the court's approval, may employ or authorize the employment of a professional person under section 327 or 1103 of this title, as the case may be, on any reasonable terms and conditions of employment, including on a retainer, on an hourly basis, *on a fixed or percentage fee basis,* or on a contingent fee basis. Notwithstanding such terms and conditions, the court may allow compensation different from the compensation provided under such terms and conditions after the conclusion of such employment, if such terms and conditions prove to have been improvident in light of developments not capable of being anticipated at the time of the fixing of such terms and conditions.

[*11 U.S.C. §328(a) (new text in italics)*]

The provisions in 2005 Act section 1206 are further codified by the acceptability of fixed or percentage fee arrangements by the specific reference to such arrangements by reference to Code section 328 in section 330(a).

3.9 Board Certification (2005 Act Section 415)

In section 330(a)(3) the Bankruptcy Code provides guidance regarding the relevant factors the court should consider in evaluating the amount of reasonable compensation to be awarded to a professional person. 2005 Act section 415 adds board certification or other demonstrated skill and expertise in the bankruptcy field to the existing list of factors in Code section 330(a)(3):

> (3) In determining the amount of reasonable compensation to be awarded *to an examiner, trustee under chapter 11, or professional person*, the court shall consider the nature, the extent, and the value of such services, taking into account all relevant factors, including—
>
> . . . .
>
> *(E) with respect to a professional person, whether the person is board certified or otherwise has demonstrated skill and experience in the bankruptcy field* . . . .

[*11 U.S.C. §330(a)(3) (new text in italics)*]

This amendment gives critical recognition to the importance of the programs designed to test and certify the skill of financial and other advisors to debtors and other parties in interest. It should serve as encouragement to financial professionals to continue to improve their skills and sit for the necessary examinations to attain accreditation. Now, when submitting fee requests, professionals should highlight their certification as a CIRA, CPA, CTP, or other case relevant designation.

3.10 Other Compensation Issues (2005 Act Section 232)

Code section 330(a)(1) provides that after notice to the parties in interest and the United States trustee and a hearing, the court may award reasonable compensation to a trustee, examiner or professional person. This provision has been expanded to include a consumer privacy ombudsman appointed under Code section 332 and an ombudsman appointed under Code section 333.

Code section 330(a)(1) provides the following:

> (a) (1) After notice to the parties in interest and the United States Trustee and a hearing, and subject to sections 326, 328, and 329, the court may award to a trustee, *a consumer privacy ombudsman appointed under section 332*, an examiner, *an ombudsman ap-*

pointed under section 333, or a professional person employed under section 327 or 1103—

(A) reasonable compensation for actual, necessary services rendered by the trustee, examiner, *ombudsman,* professional person, or attorney and by any paraprofessional person employed by any such person; and

(B) reimbursement for actual, necessary expenses.

. . .

[*11 U.S.C. §330(a)(1) (new text in italics)*]

Additionally, as included in the excerpt from Code section 330(a)(3) in determining the compensation awarded to an examiner, trustee under chapter 11, or professional person, the court shall consider the several factors that were listed. The 2005 Act for the first time included in the Code the examiners and trustees as well as other professionals. Prior law simply stated that "[i]n determining the amount of reasonable compensation to be awarded, the court shall . . ."

3.11 Effective Date of Changes

The provisions of the 2005 Act generally are effective for cases filed on or after October 17, 2005. All of the provisions discussed above become effective for cases filed on or after October 17, 2005 with the following exceptions: the provision for fraudulent transfers discussed in section 3.3 that is effective for petitions filed on or after April 20, 2006; the provisions for priority wage and employee benefits under section 507 are effective on or after April 20, 2005.

Chapter 4

Goods Sold in the Days Before the Petition Date

4.1 Reclamation (2005 Act Section 1227)

(a) Practice Prior to 2005 Act

Prior to the Bankruptcy Abuse Prevention and Consumer Protection Act of 2005 (2005 Act), the Bankruptcy Code provided some level of protection to sellers of goods who delivered those goods to the debtor in the days preceding the filing of the debtor's petition by incorporating state law reclamation rights, as provided by the Uniform Commercial Code (UCC), into the Bankruptcy Code in the form of section 546(c). Under current practice the reclamation may have been possible if the goods were received by the debtor within 10 days prior to the bankruptcy filing if the request was made within 20 days after the goods were delivered. However, the amendments made by the 2005 Act via amended Code section 546(c) and the inclusion of Code section 503(b)(9) dramatically change these rights.

Section 546(c) as amended provides:

> (c)(1) Except as provided in Subsection (d) of this Section and in Section 507(c), and subject to the prior rights of a holder of a security interest in such goods or the proceeds thereof, the rights and powers of the trustee under Sections 544(a), 545, 547, and 549 ~~of this title~~ are subject to ~~any statutory or common law~~ the right of a seller of goods that has sold goods to the debtor, in the ordinary course of such seller's business, to reclaim such goods if the debtor has received such goods while insolvent, *within 45 days before the date of the commencement of a case under this title*, but ~~(1)~~ such a seller may not reclaim ~~any~~ such goods unless such seller demands in writing reclamation of such goods—
>
> > (A) ~~before 10~~ *not later than 45* days after *the date of* receipt of such goods by the debtor; or
> >
> > (B) *not later than 20 days after the date of commencement of the case*, if ~~such 10-day~~ *the 45-day* period expires after the commencement of the

case.~~, before 20 days after receipt of such goods by the debtor; and~~

(2) If a seller of goods fails to provide notice in the manner described in paragraph (1), the seller still may assert the rights contained in Section 503(b)(9).

~~(2) the court may deny reclamation to a seller with such a right of reclamation that has made such a demand only if the court—~~

~~(A) grants the claim of such a seller priority as a claim of a kind specified in Section 503(b) of this title; or~~

~~(B) secures such claim by a lien.~~

[*11 U.S.C. §546(c) (new text in italics)*]

(b) The UCC No Longer Governs

An example may be in order. In *In re Georgetown Steel Company, LLC,*[1] the seller of goods was disputing the status of its reclamation claim regarding 12 supersacks of silicomanganes (SMI). There, the court determined that reclamation was a state law right, and thus, to prevail, the seller must prove up not only the timely written notice requirement contained in Code section 546(c), but also the elements of the state law right: (1) that the goods sold to the debtor on credit were of a type within the ordinary course of business of both parties; (2) that the debtor was insolvent pursuant to the bankruptcy code at the time of delivery of the goods; and (3) that the debtor was still in the possession of the goods or that the goods were not in the hands of a good faith purchaser at the time the demand for reclamation was received.[2] In that case, the seller was unable to prove that the debtor had possession of the goods or that they were not in the hands of a good faith purchaser, thus the seller could not prevail.[3] The replacement of the words *any statutory or common law* with the word "the" in Code section 546(c)(1) appears to change the outcome of this case by rendering the possession requirement moot.

(c) Rights of Reclamation as Amended

What if the seller in *Georgetown Steel* had prevailed? Former section 546(c)(2) gave the court the ability to deny reclamation (that is, not require the debtor to return the goods) where the elements of reclamation were shown if the court granted the seller either a lien in

[1] 318 B.R. 336 (Bankr. S.C. 2004).
[2] *Id.* at 339.
[3] *Id.* at 340.

property to secure its claim or granted a priority claim for the value of the goods. The elimination of former Code section 546(c)(2) in its entirety seems to divest the court of any option: If the seller shows that the goods were sold within 45 days of the commencement of the case to an insolvent debtor, and that a written demand was timely made, the seller appears to have an absolute right to reclaim the goods. How this will work with the definition of Property of the Estate as described by Code section 541 and the Automatic Stay provided by Code section 362 is yet to be seen. The first instances of litigation may well come when the debtor seeks to sell the goods as part of a larger parcel of goods free and clear of liens and interests pursuant to Code section 363.

4.2 Within 20 Days—De Facto Critical Vendors? (2005 Act Section 1227)

The reality is that in most cases, asset-based financing provides a prior perfected lien on most goods such that the right of reclamation is rendered moot. Furthermore, where a lien does not act to moot the reclamation rights, many vendors fail to provide the timely written notice.[4] So, why is there such concern about goods sold in the days immediately before the filing? The right to reclaim, and thus potentially put a serious dent in the debtor's ability to operate, is one answer. Another answer is found in new Code section 546(c)(2) which refers to section 503(b)(9) granting administrative expense status for:

> *(9) the value of any goods received by the debtor within 20 days before the date of commencement of a case under this title in which the goods have been sold to the debtor in the ordinary course of such debtor's business.*

[*11 U.S.C. §503(b)(9) (new text in italics)*]

This provision, in essence, appears to deem all vendors delivering goods within 20 days of the petition date "critical." Thus, as a result of this provision, it will become increasingly critical that the debtor not order any goods for product lines or stores that will be shut down at, or immediately after, the filing of the petition, which will require additional planning on the part of the debtor and its advisors to avoid unnecessary administrative expenses.

---

[4] Query, however, whether the increased time to provide that notice, and the absence of the requirement that the seller show that the goods are in the possession of either the debtor or an entity that is not a good faith purchaser, taken with the absolute right to reclaim, will increase the instances of reclamation demands.

4.3 Effective Date of Changes

The provisions of the 2005 Act generally are effective for cases filed on or after October 17, 2005. All of the provisions discussed in this chapter become effective for cases filed on or after October 17, 2005.

Chapter 5

Chapter 11 Plan of Reorganization

5.1 Introduction

Numerous provisions of the Bankruptcy Abuse Prevention and Consumer Protection Act of 2005 (2005 Act) will affect the chapter 11 plan process. This chapter explores some of the more important provisions of both the previously existing law and the 2005 revisions that affect the plan process. Even though all the effects of the 2005 Act on the chapter 11 plan process are not known at the writing of this publication, without a doubt the changes will significantly affect plan process and a debtor's ability to reorganize.

5.2 The Exclusive Period in Which to File a Plan (2005 Act Section 411)

(a) Practice Prior to 2005 Act

Code section 1121 addressed the timing for filing a plan of reorganization and soliciting votes on the same. Specifically, Code section 1121(b) provided that "[e]xcept as otherwise provided in this section, only the debtor may file a plan until after 120 days after the date of the order for relief under this chapter."[1] Moreover, Code section 1121(c)(3) established that a debtor had an additional exclusive period of 180 days within which to solicit acceptances for its plan.[2] These provisions have been commonly referred to as the "exclusive" periods.

Code section 1121(d) authorized the court to extend the exclusive periods and in fact, prior to the 2005 Act, courts routinely extended a debtor's exclusive periods. Recent examples include: *UAL Corporation, et al.* [Case No. 02-B-48191 (Bankr. N.D. Ill.) (current exclusivity extension of over 25 months in the aggregate)]; and *Armstrong World Industries, Inc., et al.* [Case No. 00-04471 (Bankr. D. Del) (current exclusivity extension of over 40 months)]. Both *UAL* and *Armstrong* are extreme examples of the amounts of time debtors have been allowed to formulate and solicit votes for a plan.

---

[1] 11 U.S.C. §1121(b).
[2] 11 U.S.C. §1121(c)(3).

(b) Changes Enacted

In contrast to the previous provisions, the 2005 Act significantly limits a debtor's ability to obtain extensions of the exclusive period to file a plan and solicit acceptances to a maximum of 18 months and 20 months respectively. Specifically, Code section 1121(d) has been amended to provide as follows:

> (1) *Subject to paragraph (2),* on request of a party in interest made within the respective periods specified in subsections (b) and (c) of this section and after notice and a hearing, the court may for cause reduce or increase the 120-day period or the 180-day period referred to in this section.
>
> (2) *(A) The 120-day period specified in paragraph (1) may not be extended beyond a date that is 18 months after the date of the order for relief under this chapter.*
>
> *(B) The 180-day period specified in paragraph (1) may not be extended beyond a date that is 20 months after the date of the order for relief under this chapter.*

[*11 U.S.C. §1121(d) (new text in italics)*]

Thus, under the revisions, a debtor (1) cannot obtain extensions of the period when it has the sole right to file a plan beyond 18 months after its bankruptcy filing, and (2) cannot obtain the sole right to solicit acceptances of a plan beyond 20 months after bankruptcy filing. This is a significant change from previous law which imposed no limit on the number of extensions.

(c) Impact of Changes

Of all the changes contained in the 2005 Act that affect plans, none are expected to have a greater impact than the changes to Code section 1121 and exclusivity. Under the previously existing provisions of the Code, debtors expected to have time necessary to address operational issues in order to be in a position to formulate a feasible plan of reorganization. Even if the process took more than the initial exclusivity period, bankruptcy courts routinely granted extensions well beyond the initial 120/180 days. The *UAL* and *Armstrong World Industries* cases are two examples of the type of leniency that bankruptcy courts have given debtors to correct problems so they may formulate a plan. For example, in *UAL*, the debtor needed additional time to address numerous labor issues that have affected the company's ability to emerge from bankruptcy. Similarly, in *Armstrong*, the debtor needed additional time to address asbestos claims.

Under the revisions in the 2005 Act, a debtor will have no more than 18 months of plan exclusivity to address the issues necessary to formulate a plan of reorganization. As a result, debtors will try to do as much planning and address as many issues as possible prior to filing chapter 11. If a debtor cannot file and solicit votes on a plan within the allotted times, it cannot prevent creditors from proposing their own plans. Of course, the ability to propose a plan is not the same thing as the ability to confirm it. The consensus building process of chapter 11 will be by the potential loss of the ability to ensure negotiations through use of continued exclusivity. Similarly, the ability to terminate exclusivity even without a showing of cause may have the effect of stimulating more intense negotiation and could possibly expedite the process.

One unintended consequence of the changes to the exclusivity provisions could be more chapter 11 liquidations. Each party in a bankruptcy case has a different interest and therefore a different view of the best possible outcome. A debtor typically will have to look at the world through the eyes of all constituencies in order to develop a plan that can be confirmed and supported by creditors. Creditors on the other hand understandably may have a myopic view of the case and only look to what is best for themselves. This different view of the case may lead a creditor to the view that a liquidation is better for creditors, notwithstanding the loss of jobs for employees. When a debtor could maintain exclusivity, it had the ability to leverage its view of a case and present its plan to creditors for a vote. Congress' decision to change the playing field with limited exclusivity could lead to more liquidations which is contrary to the *rehabilitation* concept the U.S. bankruptcy laws were designed to facilitate and have modeled for the rest of the world.

5.3 Treatment of Taxes Under a Plan (2005 Act Section 710)

(a) Practice Prior to 2005 Act

Code section 1129 addresses the requirements for confirmation of a plan. Specifically, Code section 1129(a)(9)(C) deals with tax claims. Under former Code section 1129(a)(9)(C), a debtor could provide deferred payments to a taxing authority over a period not to exceed six years after such taxes were assessed. This provision provided flexibility for debtors to address tax deficiencies, but was limited to unsecured priority tax claims. [*See, e.g., United States v. T.M. Bldg. Products Ltd.*, 231 B.R. 364, 370 (S.D. Fla. 1998) ("Section 1129(a)(9)(C) requires a Chapter 11 plan to provide for the payment of the priority taxes specified in §507(a)(8) of the Code. This subsection, by making reference to §507(a)(8), specifically concerns the treatment to be afforded the **unsecured claims** of governmental units.").] Accordingly, under the prior provisions, only unsecured claims were afforded priority status, and secured claims were treated consistently with other secured creditors under the plan. [*Id.* ("If a Notice of Federal Tax Lien is recorded before the petition in bankruptcy is filed, the creditor is classified as "secured" and the priority rules of §507(a)(8) do not apply to that secured claim.")] As will be discussed further in this section, these provisions have changed with the 2005 Act.

(b) Changes Enacted

The 2005 Act amends Code section 1129(a)(9) to address payment of claims of governmental units. Revised Code section 1129(a)(9) contemplates that the covered tax claims must be paid within *five years* from the commencement of the bankruptcy case (actually, from the entry of the order for relief which can be later than commencement in an involuntary case). The 2005 Act added Code section 511 to the Code, requiring that the interest rate on tax claims be the rate applicable to the tax claim by nonbankruptcy law determined as of the month of confirmation, and that the treatment of the tax claim be no less favorable than the best treatment afforded unsecured claims. The amended Code section 1129(a)(9) reads as follows:

> (C) with respect to a claim of a kind specified in section 507(a)(8) of this title, the holder of such claim will receive on account of such claim *regular installment* payments *in cash*—
>
> > *(i)* of a *total* value, as of the effective date of the plan, equal to the allowed amount of such claim;
> >
> > *(ii) over a period ending not later than 5 years after the date of the order for relief under section 301, 302, or 303; and*
> >
> > *(iii) in a manner not less favorable than the most favored nonpriority unsecured claim provided for by the plan (other than cash payments made to a class of creditors under section 1122(b)); and*
>
> *(D) with respect to a secured claim which would otherwise meet the description of an unsecured claim of a governmental unit under section 507(a)(8), but for the secured status of that claim, the holder of that claim will receive on account of that claim, cash payments, in the same manner and over the same period, as prescribed in subparagraph (C).*

[*11 U.S.C. §1129(a)(9) (new text in italics)*]

(c) Impact of Changes

The revisions to Code section 1129(a)(9)(C) as well as the addition of Code section 503(b)(9) granting vendors an administrative expense for goods delivered in the ordinary course of business 20 days prior to bankruptcy will affect the chapter 11 plan process. Specifically, debtors now have to factor in heightened priorities for taxes and for selected trade vendors. For example, a debtor must now consider the impact that tax claims with potentially higher interest rates based on punitive statutes will have on plan feasibility given the payment requirements in Code sections 1129(a)(9) and 511, for both priority and secured tax claims.

5.4 Treatment of Charitable Property (2005 Act Section 1221)

Code section 1129(a)(16) has been added to provide:

> *All transfers of property of the plan shall be made in accordance with any applicable provisions of non-bankruptcy law that govern the transfer of property by a corporation or trust that is, business, or commercial corporation or trust.*

[*11 U.S.C. §1129(a)(16) (new text in italics)*]

This new provision is intended to make clear that state law pertaining to governmental interests in not-for-profit entities continues to apply to their property in bankruptcy. The dispute this new provision addresses was in evidence in cases dealing with, for example, transfer of not-for-profit hospital assets through a bankruptcy case. *Note that Code section 1129(a)(16) is effective for all cases pending or for cases filed on or after April 20, 2005.*

(a) Impact of Changes

The 2005 Act has shifted the balance of power for nonprofit debtors. Specifically, section 363(d) has been amended to provide that a trustee or debtor may use, sell or lease property only in accordance with nonbankruptcy law that governs the transfer by a nonprofit corporation. Prior to the provisions, Code section 363 did not impose such a restriction and a nonprofit debtor could argue that it was free to use or sell its property regardless of state law restrictions. In addition to the changes to Code section 363(d), the 2005 Act also added Code section 1129(a)(16), which now requires that before a bankruptcy court can confirm a plan of reorganization for a nonprofit corporation, any transfers under the plan must be in accordance with applicable nonbankruptcy law governing such corporation. As a result, regardless of creditor support for a plan, a nonprofit debtor must comply with the applicable nonbankruptcy law.

5.5 Plan Modification (2005 Act Section 321)

Code section 1127 addresses modifications to plans and has also been amended. Specifically, a new subsection (f) has been added, which provides:

> *(f) (1) Sections 1121 through 1128 and the requirements of section 1129 apply to any modifications under subsection (a).*
>
> *(2) The plan, as modified, shall become the plan only after there has been disclosure under section 1125 as the court may direct, notice and a hearing, and such modification is approved.*

[*11 U.S.C. §1127(f) (new text in italics)*]

The revisions to Code section 1127 provide restrictions for debtors that need to modify a plan of reorganization prior to confirmation. Section 1127(f) provides that any modifications under Code section 1127(a) (which applies to preconfirmation modifications) must comply with Code sections 1121 through 1128 and the requirements of Code section 1129. Moreover, the modified plan can only become the actual plan after notice and a hearing and the modification is approved.

(a) Impact of Changes

The impact of the addition of Code section 1127(f) will be more procedural and administrative than substantive. Code section 1127(f) does make clear, however, that any modified plan must comply with the confirmation requirements of Code section 1129 and can only be approved by the bankruptcy court after adequate notice and opportunity for a hearing.

The revisions to Code section 1127 provide restrictions for debtors that need to modify a plan of reorganization prior to confirmation. Section 1127(f) provides that any modifications under Code section 1127(a) (which applies to preconfirmation modifications) must comply with Code sections 1121 through 1128 and the requirements of Code section 1129. Moreover, the modified plan can only become the actual plan after notice and a hearing and the modification is approved. The impact of the addition of Code section 1127(f) will be more procedural and administrative than substantive. Code section 1127(f) does make clear, however, that any modified plan must comply with the confirmation requirements of Code section 1129 and can only be approved by the bankruptcy court after adequate notice and opportunity for a hearing.

5.6 Disclosure Statement (2005 Act Section 408)

Code section 1125 addresses postpetition disclosure and solicitations and primarily addresses the requirements for disclosure statements. The changes to section 1125 should be considered when drafting a chapter 11 plan. The primary changes to section 1125 that affect plan considerations are found in Code sections 1125(a)(1) and (g). These changes require that for a disclosure statement to contain "adequate information," it now must also include a discussion of the potential material federal tax consequences of the plan to the debtor, any successor to the debtor, and a hypothetical investor typical of the holders of claims or interests in the case. Also, in a prepackaged plan, a prepetition solicitation is validated if it complied with applicable nonbankruptcy law.

Code section 1125(a)(1) has been amended as follows:

> (1) "adequate information" means information of a kind, and in sufficient detail, as far as is reasonably practicable in light of the nature and history of the debtor and the condition of the debtor's books and records, *including a discussion of the potential material Federal tax consequences of the plan to the debtor, any successor to the debtor, and a hypothetical investor typical of the holders of claims or interests in the case,* that would enable *such* a hypothetical investor of the relevant class to make an informed judgment about the plan, but adequate information need not include such information about any other possible or proposed plan *and in determining whether a disclosure statement provides adequate information, the court shall consider the complexity of the case, the benefit of additional information to creditors and other parties in interest, and the cost of providing additional information;*

[*11 U.S.C. §1125(a)(1) (new text in italics)*]

Section 1125(g) has been added to the Code and affects prepackaged plans of reorganization. Specifically, new Code section 1125(g) provides as follows:

> *(g) Notwithstanding subsection (b), an acceptance or rejection of the plan may be solicited from a holder of a claim or interest if such solicitation complies with applicable nonbankruptcy law and if such holder was solicited before the commencement of the case in a manner complying with applicable nonbankruptcy law.*

[*11 U.S.C. §1125(g) (new text in italics)*]

(a) Impact of Changes

The revisions to Code section 1125(a)(1) provide further definition to what is required by a disclosure statement while at the same time providing bankruptcy courts flexibility when considering the approval of a disclosure statement. First, Code section 1125(a)(1) now expressly requires that a disclosure statement must provide a discussion of "potential material Federal tax consequences of the plan to the debtor, any successor to the debtor, and a hypothetical investor typical of the holders of claims or interests in the case . . ." Accordingly, a debtor (or plan proponent) must provide sufficient disclosures regarding the tax consequences of its plan.

Second, Code section 1125(a)(1) provides bankruptcy courts with flexibility in approving disclosure statements. The bankruptcy court is directed to "consider the complexity of the case, the benefit of additional information to creditors and other parties in interest, and the cost of providing additional information." In essence, the bankruptcy court can now weigh the benefit of the information to be provided with the cost of providing that information. In particular, the flexibility in Code section 1125(a)(1) can be beneficial to smaller debtors. The compilation and analysis of the information needed for a disclosure statement can be expensive and time-consuming. Such time and expense may outweigh the benefit provided by such information. In these situations, Code section 1125(a)(1) now allows the court to conduct a cost-benefit analysis when determining whether a disclosure statement has adequate information.

Changes to Code section 1125(g) provide clarification with respect to continued solicitation of claim holders once a case has been filed. Specifically, Code section 1125(g) makes it clear that solicitation may continue after commencement of the case as long as the solicitation prior to the commencement of the case was in accordance with applicable nonbankruptcy law. This basically allows a solicitation to continue postpetition if it was in accordance with applicable nonbankruptcy law prepetition.

5.7 Administrative Expenses (2005 Act Section 1227)

The 2005 Act included relatively significant changes to Code section 503, including the expansion or introduction of new categories of administrative expense claims. These new or expanded administrative expense claims will have to be considered when formulating a plan of reorganization. In particular, the addition of Code section 503(b)(9) that provides for administrative expense treatment for the value of any goods received by the debtor within 20 days before the commencement of the bankruptcy case is anticipated to have a significant impact on the funds needed in order to have a feasible plan of reorganization. New section 503(b)(9) provides as follows:

> (b) After notice and a hearing, there shall be allowed administrative expenses, other than claims allowed under section 502(f) of this title including—
>
> . . .
>
> *(9) the value of any goods received by the debtor within 20 days before the date of commencement of a case under this title in which the goods have been sold to the debtor in the ordinary course of such debtor's business.*

[*11 U.S.C. §503(b)(9)) (new text in italics)*]

(a) Impact of Changes

Similarly, debtors will need to consider the impact of Code section 503(b)(9), which 503(b)(9) provides for a priority claim for "the value of any goods received by the debtor within 20 days before the date of commencement of a case under this title in which the goods have been sold to the debtor in the ordinary course of such debtor's business." Code section 503(b)(9), however, does not address the timing of such payment. While it is conceivable that a debtor could seek permission to pay such claims during the chapter 11 case, the Code does not require such payment at any time before confirmation. In order to confirm a plan, section 1129(a)(9)(A) requires that claims of the kind specified in Code section 507(a)(2) (which includes administrative expense claims under section 503(b)) be paid in cash equal to the amount of the claim. Accordingly, a debtor must make provision for payment of Code section 503(b)(9) claims if it wants to confirm its plan. Prior to the 2005 Act, this type of claim would usually have been general unsecured claims. As a result, depending on how much the debtor may have purchased in the days leading up to the bankruptcy case, the effect of the addition of Code section 503(b)(9) may end up being very significant.

5.8 Leases—Section 365 (2005 Act Section 404)

Another revision to the Code that will affect the chapter 11 plan process is the change to section 365(d)(4). Specifically, a debtor must assume or reject unexpired commercial realty leases within 120 days of a bankruptcy filing, or within 210 days of a bankruptcy filing, if the court permits such extensions. The deadlines under the prior law were an initial 60 days with potentially unlimited extensions to move to assume or reject. No extension beyond 210 days is permitted, unless the lessor consents in writing. In addition, a debtor can no longer retain the ability to assume or reject a realty lease after a plan has been confirmed. The revisions provide:

> (4) *(A) Subject to subparagraph (B), an unexpired lease of nonresidential real property under which the debtor is the lessee shall be* deemed rejected, and the trustee shall immediately surrender *that* nonresidential real property to the lessor, *if the trustee does not assume or reject the unexpired lease by the earlier of—*
>
> > *(i) the date that is 120 days after the date of the order for relief; or*
> >
> > *(ii) the date of the entry of an order confirming a plan.*
>
> *(B) (i) The court may extend the period determined under subparagraph (A), prior to 90 the expiration of the 120-day period, for 90 days on the motion of the trustee or lessor for cause.*
>
> > *(ii) If the court grants an extension under clause (i), the court may grant a subsequent extension only upon prior written consent of the lessor in each instance.*

[*11 U.S.C. §365(d)(4) (new text in italics)*]

(a) Impact of Changes

Similarly, with the revisions to Code section 365(d)(4) retail debtors will have the additional pressure of having to make decisions with respect to nonresidential real property leases earlier in their cases. For a retail debtor, such a decision can significantly affect its reorganization. The question will be whether the maximum 210-day extension (without landlord consent) is sufficient to allow a debtor to determine which of its locations it should retain as part of a reorganization plan. The 210-day period under Code section 365(d)(4) can effectively shorten the time a debtor has to formulate a plan, and the two-year administrative expense allowance (see section 2.2 of this publication) on improvidently assumed leases that are subsequently rejected creates yet another potentially substantial economic hurdle to confirmation of a feasible plan. A debtor will not want to take the risk of assuming leases that eventually will not be a part of its reorganization. As a result, a retail debtor may be forced to formulate and implement a plan before the 210-day period expires or incur obligations that may ultimately impair the financial recovery for its nonlessor creditors.

5.9 Effective Date of Changes

The provisions of the 2005 Act generally are effective for cases filed on or after October 17, 2005. The only provision discussed above that does goes into effect prior to October 17, 2005 is Code section 1129(a)(16), which was effective for all cases pending or cashed filed on or after April 20, 2005, the date the 2005 Act was enacted.

Chapter 6

Composition and Selection of Creditors' Committees

6.1 Introduction

Several changes from the Bankruptcy Abuse Prevention and Consumer Protection Act of 2005 (2005 Act) will have an effect on creditors' committees, including the means by which creditors' committees are composed and the process by which changes are made to the membership of committees. This chapter discusses these changes as well as the impact they will have.

6.2 Committee Reconstitution and Treatment of Constituent Members (2005 Act Sections 405 and 432)

(a) Practice Prior to 2005 Act

Prior to its deletion in 1986, Code section 1102(c) provided for the court to order a change in the membership or size of a committee appointed under Code section 1102(a), if the court determined that the membership of the committee was not representative of the different kinds of claims or interests to be represented.[1] The 1986 amendments that repealed Code section 1102(c) also expanded the role of the Office of the U.S. Trustee (U.S. trustee) in chapter 11 cases and provided that the U.S. trustee shall appoint a committee of creditors of unsecured claims and may appoint additional committees of creditors or equity security holders as the U.S. trustee deems appropriate.[2] The courts have reviewed the U.S. trustees' decisions with respect to

---

[1] 11 U.S.C. §1102(c) (repealed).
[2] 11 U.S.C. §1102(a)(1).

committee composition issues either *de novo* or under an abuse of discretion standard.[3]

Even though there has not been a hard-and-fast rule for appointment of a committee, it has generally been accepted (and contemplated by Code section 1102(b)(1)) that the U.S. trustee appoint the seven largest unsecured creditors to a committee. In several situations, especially in larger cases, the U. S. trustee has appointed committees larger than seven. In addition, U.S. trustees typically have tried to have representatives of both bondholders and trade vendors on committees to balance the interests of unsecured creditors.

As will be discussed in the following sections, several provisions introduced by the 2005 Act make significant changes in committees and how they operate.

(b) Changes Enacted

There are a number of new changes that will affect creditors' committees and their operations. The primary changes are found in Code section 1102. Specifically, new sections 1102(a)(4) and (b)(3) have been added. The first change is that the power of a bankruptcy court to order a change in committee membership to ensure adequate representation is now clear. The second major change relates to the communications with and the type of information required to be provided to unsecured creditors who are not on the committee but are represented by the committee.

Code section 1102(a)(4) provides:

---

[3] *Compare In re Sharon Steel Corp.*, 100 B.R. 767, 785 (Bankr. W.D. Pa. 1989) and *In re Texaco*, 79 B.R. 560 (Bankr. S.D.N.Y. 1987) (both suggesting that the *de novo* review is applicable), with *In re FastMart Convenience Stores, Inc.*, 265 B.R. 427 (Bankr. E.D. Va. 2001); *In re First Republic Bank Corp.*, 95 B.R. 58, 60 (Bankr. N.D. Tex. 1988) and *In re Columbia Gas Sys.*, 133 B.R. 174 (Bankr. D. Del. 1991) (suggesting that an abuse of discretion standard may apply). *See generally* Bruce H. White, *A Question of Authority: Can the Bankruptcy Court alter the composition of creditors' committees appointed by the U.S. Trustees?*, 16 Am. Bankr. Inst. J. 22 (July/Aug. 1997). The bankruptcy court in *In re Victory Markets, Inc.*, 196 B.R. 1 (Bankr. N.D.N.Y. 1995), determined that repeal of section 1102(c) precluded bankruptcy court review of the U.S. Trustee's decision in appointing committee members. Two district courts, sitting as appellate courts, have rejected the argument that Congress precluded a review of U.S. Trustees' decisions by repealing section 1102(c). *See In re Voluntary Purchasing Groups, Inc.*, No. 4:96CV396, 1997 WL 155407 (E.D. Tex. Mar. 21, 1997); *In re Lykes Bros. Steamships Co., Inc.*, 200 B.R. 933 (M.D. Fla. 1996).

Note: Lawrence R. Ahern III is co-author of the Thomson/West publication, *2005 Bankruptcy Reform Legislation with Analysis*, part of which formed the basis for this chapter and is printed here with permission. Thanks to David W. Houston IV for his contribution to this chapter and to Mr. Houston and Darlene T. Marsh for their review of the manuscript.

(4) On request of a party in interest and after notice and a hearing, the court may order the United States trustee to change the membership of a committee appointed under this subsection, if the court determines that the changes are necessary to ensure adequate representation of creditors or equity security holders. The court may order the United States trustee to increase the number of members of a committee to include a creditor that is a small business concern (as described in section 3(a)(1) of the Small Business Act); if the court determines that the creditor holds claims (of the kind represented by the committee) the aggregate amount of which, in comparison to the annual gross revenue of that creditors, is disproportionately large.

Code section 1102(b)(3) provides:

(3) A committee appointed under subsection (a) shall—

(A) provide access to information for creditors who—

(i) hold claims of the kind represented by that committee; and

(ii) are not appointed to the committee;

(B) solicit and receive comments from the creditors described in subparagraph (A); and

(C) be subject to a court order that compels any additional report or disclosure to be made to the creditors described in subparagraph (A).

[*11 U.S.C. §1102(a)(4) and (b)(3) (new text in italics)*]

(c) Impact of Changes

The amendments to the Code have changed how committees are composed and the process by which changes are made to their membership. In addition, creditors' committees will be required to disclose information to the constituencies that those committees represent, and they will be required to solicit and receive comments from creditors in the class represented by the committees. The net effect of the changes is that (1) the bankruptcy court will have a more significant role in determining the composition of creditors' committees and (2) the previous practice regarding delivery of material nonpublic information into the possession of the committee is altered. The amendments create a level of complexity and additional costs for committees, and hence, chapter 11 debtors as well.

Committee Composition

The 2005 Act alters the way in which committees are formed. The court has a much more direct role in the process and can order changes to the committee membership as well as the appointment of a small business concern to the committee. However, the question of the standard of review of the actions of the U.S trustee in making appointments and determining adequate representation is not clear under the amendments. Will it be *de novo* or under an abuse of discretion standard consistent with the Administrative Procedures Act?

As discussed above, the Code simply provided that the U.S. trustee shall appoint a committee of creditors of unsecured claims and may appoint additional committees of creditors or equity security holders as the U.S. trustee deems appropriate. The 2005 Act, however, now expressly provides that the court may order the U.S. trustee to change the membership of a committee appointed, if the court determines that the change is necessary to ensure adequate representation of creditors or equity security holders.[4] Interestingly, in contrast to the prior version of section 1102(c), the amendment does not address, at least explicitly, the issue of the size of the committee nor does it address whether multiple committees would be appropriate.[5]

The Small Business Concern Provision

The 2005 Act also affects committee composition. Pursuant to Code section 1102(b)(1), the U.S. trustee appointed the committee from the holders of the largest unsecured claims against the debtor. At times, depending on the pool of eligible committee members, the U.S. Trustee may appoint a smaller or larger committee (although typically an odd number is appointed in order to deal with voting issues and avoid stalemates).

Now, under the 2005 Act, the bankruptcy court may order the U.S. trustee to increase the number of members of a committee to include a creditor that is a "small business concern" if the court determines that the creditor holds claims of the kind represented by the committee and the aggregate amount of the claims, in comparison to the annual gross revenue of that creditor, is disproportionately large.[6] This type of creditor might not otherwise be appointed to a committee and may not have the experience or expertise with respect to the financial issues that come before a committee. This will add to the job

---

[4] 11 U.S.C. §1102(a)(4).

[5] With respect to multiple committees, the courts focused on the adequacy of representation of all interests concerned as well as the additional costs involved with multiple committees. *See, e.g., In re Sharon Steel Corp.*, 100 B.R. at 776.

[6] 11 U.S.C. §1102(a)(4).

of the committee counsel in terms of synthesizing the various points of view of the creditors on the committee and articulating a relatively consensual view to the court (and, as discussed later in this chapter, to other creditors not on the committee). Appointment of committees comprised of other than the largest creditors is usually a situation that arises when different constituencies such as trade debt, landlord, and institutional debt holders, are all on a single committee (sometimes with a 4-3-2 structure for example).

Although the statute does not make this explicit, it is likely that the small business concern desirous of serving on the committee will initially contact the U.S. trustee and request appointment. If the U.S. trustee (who likely will consult with the debtors and the committee) does not appoint that creditor to the committee, the creditor could file a motion with the court seeking an order directing the U.S. trustee to so appoint that creditor to the committee. As a tactical matter, the debtor and the committee may not want to make public their opposition to such a motion as they may have to live with the creditor on the committee going forward. Moreover, assuming there are a number of small business concerns that are interested, it may be that the race goes to the swift and that there will be some jockeying for position on this issue.

The additional power of the bankruptcy court and the additional complexities raised by the different experience level, agenda, and motivation of the small business concern will only add to the tasks of committee counsel.

Eligibility Issues

Members of a committee owe a fiduciary duty to the constituencies that the committee represents. This does not mean that they cannot act in their own economic interest, but that they cannot do so when they are supposed to be acting as fiduciaries for an entire class. In certain cases, the courts have held that competitors or active litigants may not sit on a committee as they could not discharge that fiduciary duty, and other cases have gone the other way.[7] The U.S. trustee usually focuses on the ability of a creditor to discharge this fiduciary duty in determining whether to appoint that creditor to the committee, but recognizes that adversity with a debtor is not a basis to be excluded from the chapter 11 process since the process is intended to deal with that adversity.

One eligibility issue that may arise under the provisions of the 2005 Act is due to the enhanced priority for prepetition trade claims,

---

[7] *See In re Tri Mfg. & Sales Co.*, 51 B.R. 178 (Bankr. S.D. Ohio 1985); *In re Wilson Food Corp.*, 31 B.R. 272 (Bankr. W.D. Okla. 1983). *But see In re Map Int'l, Inc.*, 105 B.R. 5 (Bankr. E.D. Pa. 1989).

which could reduce the eligible pool of potential committee members. For example, new Code section 503(b)(9) provides for an additional administrative expense priority for "the value of any goods received by the debtor within 20 days before the date of commencement of a case under this title in which the goods have been sold to the debtor in the ordinary course of such debtor's business."[8] Because of the rather significant nature of this relief, one could expect a debtor to litigate the valuation issue in order to minimize what would be an additional administrative expense that would have to be paid at confirmation[9] (or sooner) and may impede the ability of a debtor in a chapter 11 case to obtain exit financing. In addition, Code section 546(c) has been modified to expand the reclamation period to 45 days before the petition date.[10] Given the additional administrative priorities for those trade vendors actively doing business with the debtor, a U.S. trustee may have to do further due diligence with respect to potential trade vendor participants on committees so as to determine whether those trade vendors would have administrative claims and how that might affect their relationship to the interests of general unsecured creditors.

Committee Operations—Disclosure Obligations

Code section 1102(b)(3) has been added to provide that a committee appointed under section 1102 shall provide access to information for creditors who hold claims of the kind represented by the committee and are not appointed to the committee. At least two issues arise from this revision. First, confidentiality concerns will be paramount as the creditors' committee will possess material, nonpublic information produced by the debtor to allow the creditors' committee to understand the debtor's business plan and reorganization strategy. Second, the disclosure obligation could create issues involving the disclosure of information otherwise protected by the attorney-client privilege between the committee counsel and the committee itself.

In many public company cases, the debtor tries to condition the transmission of detailed financial information to the committee on the entry of a protective order and/or the execution of a confidentiality agreement by committee members (and, sometimes, the committee professionals). The debtor's rationale for these conditions is the protection of material nonpublic information from dissemination, and creditors on the creditors' committee will have a fiduciary duty to protect that information. Counsel for the debtor and the committee may well seek guidance from the court at the outset of the case, detailing

---

[8] 11 U.S.C. §503(b)(9).
[9] *See* 11 U.S.C. §1129(a)(9)(A).
[10] *See* 11 U.S.C. §546(c)(1)(A).

the method and means by which this disclosure obligation is discharged by the committee. One would expect this request for guidance to include an attempt to deal with the confidential information of the debtor so as to keep creditors from attempting to gain access to this information.

Moreover, the courts have recognized the existence of the attorney-client privilege between committee counsel and the committee.[11] The bankruptcy court in *In re Baldwin-United Corp.* applied a balancing test to determine whether to require the committee to disclose privileged information to the constituent creditors.[12] Diligent committee counsel will request guidance from the bankruptcy court at the outset on this issue, so as to avoid any privilege disputes later in the case.

Committee Operations—Solicitation and Receipt of Comments

Code section 1102(b)(3)(B) adds an additional provision requiring the committee to "solicit and receive comments from creditors" of all the kinds represented by the committee. While this certainly occurs on an *ad hoc* basis through the course of a typical chapter 11 case, this new affirmative duty will require the committee to put into place procedures to address the concerns of creditors that are not on the committee. One could see the use of a Web page or other electronic media to solicit comments from creditors and to provide information to discharge the disclosure obligation discussed above. Again, one would expect that committee counsel would work with debtor's counsel to seek an order from the bankruptcy court at the outset of the case (to the extent that the case is sufficiently significant) that would include guidance as to the outlines of this particular duty.

6.3 Effective Date of Changes

The provisions of the 2005 Act generally are effective for cases filed on or after October 17, 2005. All the provisions discussed above become effective for cases filed on or after October 17, 2005.

---

[11] *See In re Baldwin-United Corp.*, 38 B.R. 802 (Bankr. S.D. Ohio 1984); *see also Marcus v. Parker (In re Subpoena Duces Tecum dated March 16, 1992)*, 978 F.2d 1159 (9th Cir. 1992).

[12] In this regard, the *Baldwin-United* court looked to the Fifth Circuit decision in the context of shareholder derivative litigation in *Garner v. Wolfinbarger*, 430 F.2d 1093 (5th Cir. 1970).

Chapter 7

Significant Changes Requiring Additional Cash Planning for Utility Service

7.1 Introduction

Section 417 of the Bankruptcy Abuse Prevention and Consumer Protection Act of 2005 (2005 Act), effective October 17, 2005, significantly modifies provisions related to utility service under amended Code section 366. While the new law still protects the debtor from termination of service by the utility, it arguably expands the rights of utilities by codifying more substantial forms of adequate assurance and disallowing forms that have been historically used, such as administrative expense priority. While courts may look to avoid radically different results from those under the prior provisions, the 2005 Act imposes a new and possibly severe financial burden on debtors at the beginning of the case by requiring debtors to provide adequate assurance in the form of cash deposits or similar forms.

Amended Code section 366 gives chapter 11 debtors 30 days instead of 20 to provide adequate assurance that is "satisfactory to the utility." The debtor and its advisors will need more careful prepetition planning to determine and provide an adequate amount of cash or debtor-in-processing (DIP) financing resources to satisfy the utilities' requirements. This amendment will likely have the most negative impact on cash flows of debtors with high utilities costs, such as multilocation retailers and manufacturers. In addition, under the new law utilities are no longer required to receive court approval to recover or set off against prepetition deposits. Finally, the meaning of the term *utility* remains uncertain under the new law. The fact that the term *utility* is not defined, particularly as it relates to telecom companies, will continue to give rise to disputes on entitlement to the protections offered under Code section 366.

7.2 Significant Changes to Utility Service (2005 Act Section 417)

(a) Practice Prior to 2005 Act

In normal operations the debtor, depending on its size and business, could use any combination of services (such as water, natural gas, electricity, sewer, telephone, Internet, paging, cable, or cellular phones, etc.) from among potentially hundreds of utility companies and other service providers. These services are critical to its successful reorganization and any interruption or termination could jeopardize reorganization efforts. Prior to its amendment, Code section 366 consisted of Code section 366(a) and (b). Under Code section 366(a), utilities were prevented from altering, refusing or discontinuing service to, or discriminating against the debtor solely on the basis of (1) commencement of a bankruptcy case or (2) an unpaid prepetition debt owed by the debtor to the utility for services rendered but not paid when due. Code section 366(b) provided the authority for the utility to "alter, refuse or discontinue service" if the debtor did not furnish "adequate assurance of payment" within 20 days from the petition date. Adequate assurance of payment for postpetition utility services could take the form of a "deposit or other security." Finally, after a party-in-interest request, notice and a hearing, the court could order "reasonable modification" of the amount necessary to provide adequate assurance of payment.

As a result of having no statutory definition of the term *adequate assurance of payment*, bankruptcy judges used their discretion on a case-by-case basis. Thus while some courts required deposits, others required no deposits where the debtor: (1) had a history of regular payment of the utility, (2) owed insignificant unpaid prepetition amounts, (3) granted the utility an administrative expense priority, and/or (4) had substantial liquid assets.

Previous Approach

As part of first-day motions the debtor's practice typically was to file a motion to provide a uniform approach to assurance of payment across all utilities. More specifically, the practice was to establish procedures to resolve requests for additional assurance. If the parties could not agree on additional assurance, the utilities objected, the debtor filed a motion for determination, and ultimately, the court held an evidentiary hearing to determine the proper assurance of payment. As a means to minimize its financial burden, the debtor would likely assert no deposit was required due to its strong historic payment record coupled with postpetition DIP financing and the administrative expense priority granted to the utility. These assurances taken together constituted adequate assurance of payment. In cases like *Adelphia*,[1] the court held "the totality of circumstances" including administrative expense priority status for a utility were sufficient to constitute assurance of payment under Code section 366.

To the extent a deposit was necessary, debtors preferred the smallest amount considered reasonable by the Court, which may have

---

[1] *In re Adelphia Bus. Solutions*, 280 B.R. 63 (Bankr. D.N.Y. 2002).

been anywhere from one to three months of average service. Averages have been based on latest usage, highest usage or a trailing 12-month calculation adjusted for new developments. Debtors have requested and been granted one large deposit for all utilities to reduce the administrative work associated with multiple deposits. Utilities have routinely objected to these debtor proposals requesting individual deposits or other forms of security for two to three months of average service, contending the other so-called protections such as administrative expense priority did not constitute "adequate assurance of payment." If called upon to rule, the court has leaned more often toward the debtor's position in this matter than toward the utilities'.

(b) Changes Enacted

The 2005 Act added section 366(c) to the Code, providing as follows:

> *(1) (A) For purposes of this subsection, the term assurance of payment means—*
>
> *(i) a cash deposit;*
>
> *(ii) a letter of credit;*
>
> *(iii) a certificate of deposit;*
>
> *(iv) a surety bond;*
>
> *(v) a prepayment of utility consumption; or*
>
> *(vi) another form of security that is mutually agreed on between the utility and the debtor or the trustee.*
>
> *(B) For purposes of this subsection an administrative expense priority shall not constitute an assurance of payment.*
>
> *(2) Subject to paragraphs (3) and (4), with respect to a case filed under chapter 11, a utility referred to in subsection (a) may alter, refuse, or discontinue utility service, if during the 30-day period beginning on the date of the filing of the petition, the utility does not receive from the debtor or the trustee adequate assurance of payment for utility service that is satisfactory to the utility.*
>
> *(3) (A) On request of a party in interest and after notice and a hearing, the court may order modification of the amount of an assurance of payment under paragraph (2).*

(B) In making a determination under this paragraph whether an assurance of payment is adequate, the court may not consider—

(i) the absence of security before the date of the filing of the petition;

(ii) the payment by the debtor of charges for utility service in a timely manner before the date of the filing of the petition; or

(iii) the availability of an administrative expense priority.

(4) Notwithstanding any other provision of law, with respect to a case subject to this subsection, a utility may recover or set off against a security deposit provided to the utility by the debtor before the date of the filing of the petition without notice or order of the court.

[*11 U.S.C. §366(c) (new text in italics)*]

As amended, Code section 366 reduces judicial discretion and inconsistent interpretation to a large degree by expressly defining what may or may not constitute an assurance of payment. The new law provides utilities with greater assurance of payment of postpetition services by adding a new subsection (c) to section 366, defining the term *assurance of payment* as:

- A cash deposit;
- Letter of credit;
- A certificate of deposit;
- A surety bond;
- A prepayment of utility consumption; or
- Another form of security that is mutually agreed on between the utility and the debtor.

The new law goes further by providing that an administrative expense priority shall not constitute an assurance of payment. Moreover, in making its determination of whether or not there is adequate assurance of payment, the court may no longer consider:

- The absence of security before the prepetition date;
- The debtor's timeliness of prepetition payments; or
- The availability of an administrative expense priority.

Furthermore, under Code section 366(c) the utility may "alter, refuse or discontinue utility service" if it does not receive adequate assurance of payment that is "satisfactory to the utility" within 30 days of the filing of a chapter 11 bankruptcy petition. Finally, the amendment allows a utility to recover or set off against a pre-petition deposit without notice or court order.

(c) Impact of Changes

New Approach

The debtor and its advisors should meet with the utility early (that is, during the first 30 days) to determine the proper amount and form of assurance that will be satisfactory to each utility. The amendment provides the debtor an additional 10 days over the previous law. This additional time may be needed by the debtor and its advisors to negotiate with each utility separately.

As part of first-day motions, the debtor and its advisors need to craft a solution with the utilities that both protects the utilities' interests in assuring payment of postpetition services and avoids as much as possible the negative impact on cash of a large deposit. One possible alternative would be to seek approval of assurance of payment in the form of an estimated weekly or monthly prepayment of utility consumption with no deposit or other form of assurance. The estimated prepay-as-you-go alternative is an acceptable form of adequate assurance of payment under the new law that will serve to minimize the financial burden in the beginning of the case. However, it is unclear whether the utilities will consider prepayment alone as satisfactory or not. (*See Supra Telecommunications* as an example of a prepayment case under the old law.) While payment history and administrative expense priority status are no longer evidence of adequate assurance, the court retains some judicial discretion. Amended Code section 366 allows the court to order "modification" of the amount necessary to provide adequate assurance of payment. The ultimate form and amount of assurance of payment acceptable to utilities and the courts will not be known until amended Code section 366 goes into effect and the courts have an opportunity to rule on the matter.

Potential Impact

Under the new law the most significant change is the careful prepetition planning needed by the debtor and its advisors to ensure adequate cash or DIP financing resources to provide assurance of payment in form and amount satisfactory to the utilities within the first 30 days of the case, or as subsequently ordered by the court. The advisors will need to perform additional analyses to reflect the cash impact in the 13-week cash flow forecast. While the amendment does not define the amount or period for which the debtor must furnish assurance of payment, the new law allows a utility to terminate service if the utility does not receive assurance of payment that is satisfactory to the utility within 30 days following the chapter 11 petition date. The new law limits judicial discretion and strongly favors the utility—which raises the question of how many months of service are necessary to reach a level of assurance of payment that is satisfactory to the utility. The request by a utility for a deposit under the prior law has varied greatly but typically has been two to three months of service plus one month prepaid. Under the new law, the court may modify the amount of an assurance of payment if the parties cannot agree on a form, an amount, or both.

The best way to illustrate the magnitude of the potential financial burden imposed by the new law on the debtor is through a well-known example. Hypothetically, if the Winn-Dixie bankruptcy case were filed in November of 2005 after the new law went into effect (rather than February 2005), the additional cash on hand to meet the new assurance of payment requirements (assuming three months of service) would be $48 million. Winn-Dixie has accounts with over 800 different utilities totaling an average of approximately $16 million per month in services.

For some debtors, the size of a DIP financing may have to be increased to provide sufficient liquidity to meet this new use of cash by the debtor and make utility deposit payments in the first month of filing. Advisors will need to work closely with DIP lenders to properly size the DIP facilities to reflect this new cash usage in the DIP budget. As previously discussed, this is especially true in the case of high utility cost debtors (for example, retailers with numerous locations or industrial companies) where the size of a cash deposit requirement or other form of assurance of payment could mean the difference between reorganization and immediate liquidation. If the debtor lacks the cash to fund a deposit, it will be faced with termination of service that could well shut down its business. In a worst case scenario, if the inability to provide postpetition assurance causes the debtor to liquidate, the recovery to general unsecured claimants may be less than under a reorganization, and the new amendment may result in utilities recovering less on prepetition claims.

Another impact could be larger prepetition claims by utilities. One source of cash for postpetition deposits is cash retained by deferring prepetition obligations. Historically, debtors kept utilities as current as possible because of the postpetition adequate assurance benefit. Thus, since prepetition payment history no longer carries weight, a debtor can file owing more to a utility, and use the cash saved to provide the postpetition assurance required. Some debtors will undoubtedly try to stretch prepetition payment to utilities as far as possible. In this case, a utility may trade its assurance of payment for postpetition service for a larger prepetition claim.

Finally, the new law provides utilities with another benefit in terms of the ability of utilities to set off cash deposits held by the utilities against prepetition debts without a court order. The utilities' ability to recover or set off the deposit will eliminate its legal costs associated with receiving court approval under the old law. Another impact of the amendment is on the area of financial reporting. For purposes of financial reporting under Statement Of Position 90-7, *Financial Reporting by Entities in Reorganization Under the Bankruptcy Code* the old law required that utilities prepetition deposits and debts were reported on a gross basis. Under the new law, the debtor and its advisors need to properly reflect the utilities' prepetition deposits and debts on a net basis.

7.3 Open Issue: Definition of Utility

One issue that remains open under the new law is the meaning of *utility*. The fact that the term *utility* is not defined, particularly as it relates to business with telecom companies, will continue to give rise to disputes on deposit entitlement because, since there is no clear answer on what constitutes a utility in the age of deregulation.

7.4 Effective Date of Changes

The changes related to utilities is effective for all petitions filed on or after October 17, 2005.

Chapter 8
Fraudulent Transfers

8.1 Introduction

The Bankruptcy Abuse Prevention and Consumer Protection Act of 2005 (2005 Act) includes changes to the fraudulent transfer provisions of the Code. There are three primary changes to the Code's fraudulent transfer laws. These changes expand the powers of a trustee in addition to adding new causes of action.

8.2 Two-Year Time Period (2005 Act Section 1402)

(a) Current Fraudulent Transfer Laws

American fraudulent transfer law derives from the so-called Statute of Elizabeth passed in 1570 in England.[1] The Statute of Elizabeth was enacted to provide a remedy to creditors in the fairly typical intentional fraudulent transfer situation in which a debtor would transfer its assets to a third-party, often a family member or close friend, and thus avoid having those assets levied upon and seized by the local sheriff when the sheriff came collecting on behalf of the creditor.

Courts and legislatures gradually came to the conclusion that a transfer could be deemed fraudulent even when actual intent could not be proved or might not even exist. Thus, in 1918, the National Conference of Commissioners on Uniform State Laws adopted the Uniform Fraudulent Conveyance Act (UFCA). UFCA attempted to correct two major deficiencies in the preceding 300 years of fraudulent conveyance law. First, UFCA attempted to provide clear, concise definitions of insolvency and the class of creditors protected by fraudulent conveyance laws. Second, UFCA set forth a theory for avoidance of transfers that could be deemed constructively fraudulent although not intentionally fraudulent. UFCA proposed that a transfer could be avoided as fraudulent when the debtor did not receive "fair consideration" for making the transfer, and at the same time, the debtor was insolvent or rendered insolvent by the transfer, or was left with such unreasonably small assets that, even if not technically insolvent, could not generally pay its debts as they came due.

---

[1] 13 Eliz., ch. 5 (1570).

Although UFCA was quickly adopted by several states, it soon became apparent that UFCA had several shortcomings as well, chief among them a lack of clear definitions for the terms utilized in UFCA. Thus, the Uniform Fraudulent Transfers Act (UFTA) was adopted as a refinement of UFCA and has become the fraudulent transfer statute utilized by the majority of states today; some states , however, still follow UFCA.

The Code also contains its own fraudulent conveyance section, section 548, which is similar to, and contains aspects of, both UFTA and UFCA. In addition to Code section 548, Code section 544 allows the debtor to use the applicable state laws to avoid a fraudulent transfer.[2]

(b) Changes Enacted

The 2005 Act has changed the Code's fraudulent transfer laws in some significant ways. The changes will undoubtedly provide more power to trustees to avoid otherwise unavoidable transfers. Specifically, Code section 548(a) has been amended to provide for, among other things, longer statutes of limitation in bringing such claims (2 years and 10 years), and for the ability to avoid certain transfers of compensation to insiders not in the ordinary course of business even if the debtor was not insolvent at the time of the transfer. The new law provides that:

> (a)(1) The trustee may avoid any transfer *(including any transfer to or for the benefit of an insider under an employment contract)* or an interest of the debtor in property, or any obligation by the debtor, that was made or incurred on or within 2 years, before the date of the filing of the petition, if the debtor voluntarily or involuntarily—
>
> (A) made such transfer or incurred such obligation with actual intent to hinder, delay or defraud an entity to which the debtor was or became, on or after the date that such transfer was made or such obligation was incurred, indebted; or
>
> (B) (i) received less than a reasonably equivalent value in exchange for such transfer or obligation; and
>
> (ii) (I) was insolvent on the date that such transfer was made or such obligation was

---

[2] 11 U.S.C. §544; *see also Bay Plastics, Inc. v. BT Comm. Corp. (In re Bay Plastics, Inc.)*, 187 B.R. 315, 322 (Bankr. C.D. Cal. 1995).

incurred, or became insolvent as a result of such transfer or obligation;

(II) was engaged in business or a transaction, or was about to engage in business or a transaction, for which any property remaining with the debtor was an unreasonably small capital;

(III) intended to incur, or believed that the debtor would incur, debts that would be beyond the debtor's ability to pay as such debts matured; *or*

(IV) made such transfer to or for the benefit of an insider, or incurred such obligation to or for the benefit of an insider, under an employment contract and not in the ordinary course of business.

[*11 U.S.C. §548(a)(1) (new text in italics)*]

(c) Impact of Changes

A trustee now has a longer look-back period for determining if a fraudulent transfer occurred. For example, under previously existing Code section 548 provisions, a trustee could only seek to avoid a transfer if it occurred less than a year before the filing of the bankruptcy. Under the 2005 Act, the trustee now can look back for a two-year period. This obviously gives a trustee the ability to look at a wider range of transactions.

As a practical matter, the changes to Code section 548(a) may not really expand a trustee's power. For example, under Code section 544(b) of the Code (unchanged by the 2005 Act), a trustee has the ability to avoid any transfer or obligation incurred that is voidable under applicable nonbankruptcy law by a creditor holding an unsecured claim against the debtor. Most states had a longer statute of limitations than the one-year period under the old Code section 548. Accordingly, most trustees had to use Code section 544(b), looking to applicable state law to avoid a transfer. Now under revised Code section 548(a), the trustee can use either the Code's fraudulent transfer provisions (with a two-year look back) or applicable state law (with the applicable statute of limitations particular to the state).

8.3 Transfer to Insiders

Section 548(a), as discussed in 3.3, has been amended to give the debtor-in-possession or trustee the ability to avoid certain transfers of compensation to insiders not in the ordinary course of business even if the debtor was not insolvent at the time of the transfer.

(a) Impact of Changes

Code section 548(a)(1) has also been expanded to include transfers to insiders outside the ordinary course of business in which the debtor received less than reasonably equivalent value in exchange. This provides another tool for a trustee to go after questionable payments to insiders without having to establish the solvency of the debtor.

8.4 Ten-Year Time Period (2005 Act Section 1401)

In addition to the changes to Code section 548(a), the 2005 Act added a new Code section 548(e), which provides:

> *(e) (1) In addition to any transfer that the trustee may otherwise avoid, the trustee may avoid any transfer of an interest of the debtor in property that was made on or within 10 years before the date of the filing of the petition if—*
>
> *(A) such transfer was made to a self-settled trust or similar device;*
>
> *(B) such transfer was by the debtor;*
>
> *(C) the debtor is a beneficiary of such trust or similar device; and*
>
> *(D) the debtor made such transfer with actual intent to hinder, delay, or defraud any entity to which the debtor was or became, on or after the date that such transfer was made, indebted.*
>
> *(2) For the purposes of this subsection a transfer includes a transfer made in anticipation of any money judgment settlement, civil penalty, equitable order, or criminal fine incurred by, or which the debtor believed would be incurred by—*
>
> *(A) any violation of the securities laws (as defined in section 3(a)(47) of the Securities Exchange Act of 1934 (15 U.S.C. 78c(a)(47))), any State securities laws, or any regulation or order issued under Federal securities laws of State securities laws; or*
>
> *(B) fraud, deceit, or manipulation in a fiduciary capacity or in connection with the pur-*

> *chase or sale of any security registered under section 12 of 15(d) of the Securities Exchange Act of 1934 (15 U.S.C. 781 and 78o(d)) or under section 6 of the Securities Act of 1933 (15 U.S.C. 77f)*

[*11 U.S.C. §548(e) (new text in italics)*]

(a) Impact of Changes

Perhaps the most significant change to Code section 548 is the addition of section 548(e) which is designed to address the quintessential case in which a debtor plans for the worst and sets up a self-settled trust. In essence, a debtor transfers all assets out of its possession, yet retains an interest as a beneficiary of the trust. Prior to the addition of Code section 548(e), a trustee was usually powerless to avoid such a transfer. However, under revised Code section 548(e), the trustee can avoid such a transaction that has occurred as far back as 10 years prior to the bankruptcy filing. A key point is the debtor must have had the intention to delay or defraud creditors. This will certainly be an area of litigation for trustees as they attempt to enhance estate values. It should be cautioned, however, that actually recovering the transferred property from the trust can be difficult at best if the law of the country where the trust assets rest does not recognize U.S. law.

8.5 Effective Date of Changes

The provisions of the 2005 Act are generally effective for cases filed on or after October 17, 2005. The changes to Code section 548(a)(1) dealing with transfer to an insider and the addition of Code section 548(e) became effective on April 20, 2005, the day the 2005 Act was enacted. These changes are effective for any cases filed on or after that day. The change in Code section 548(a)(1) expanding the look-back to two years only applies to cases filed on or after April 20, 2006.

Chapter 9

Changes in Amounts and Order of Priority Claims

9.1 Introduction

The Bankruptcy Abuse Prevention and Consumer Protection Act of 2005 (2005 Act) moved the claim for domestic support obligations from seventh priority to first priority. The priorities previously numbered first through sixth were changed to second through seventh priorities, and a new tenth priority was added. In addition, the monetary limit for wages and employee benefits was increased.

9.2 First Priority: Domestic Support Obligations (2005 Act Section 212)

The first priority claim is now a claim for domestic support obligations. Code section 507(a)(1) provides:

> (a) The following expenses and claims have priority in the following order:
>
> (1) First,
>
>> *(A) Allowed unsecured claims for domestic support obligations that, as of the date of the filing of the petition in a case under this title, are owed to or recoverable by a spouse, former spouse, or child of the debtor, or such child's parent, legal guardian, or responsible relative, without regard to whether the claim is filed by such person or is filed by a governmental unit on behalf of such person, on the condition that funds received under this paragraph by a governmental unit under this title after the date of the filing of the petition shall be applied and distributed in accordance with applicable nonbankruptcy law.*
>>
>> *(B) Subject to claims under subparagraph (A), allowed unsecured claims for domestic support obligations that, as of the date of the filing of the petition, are assigned by a spouse, former spouse, child of the debtor, or such child's parent, legal guardian, or responsible relative to a governmental unit*

> *(unless such obligation is assigned voluntarily by the spouse, former spouse, child, parent, legal guardian, or responsible relative of the child for the purpose of collecting the debt) or are owed directly to or recoverable by a governmental unit under applicable nonbankruptcy law, on the condition that funds received under this paragraph by a governmental unit under this title after the date of the filing of the petition be applied and distributed in accordance with applicable nonbankruptcy law.*
>
> *(C) If a trustee is appointed or elected under section 701, 702, 703, 1104, 1202, or 1302, the administrative expenses of the trustee allowed under paragraphs (1)(A), (2), and (6) of section 503(b) shall be paid before payment of claims under subparagraphs (A) and (B), to the extent that the trustee administers assets that are otherwise available for the payment of such claims.*

[*11 U.S.C. §507(a)(1) (new text in italics)*]

9.3 Fourth and Fifth Priority: Wages and Employee Benefits (2005 Act Section 1401)

Code section 507(a)(4) and (a)(5) now provide the following:

> *(4) Fourth*, allowed unsecured claims, but only to the extent of *$10,000* for each individual or corporation, as the case may be, earned within *180* days before the date of the filing of the petition or the date of the cessation of the debtor's business, whichever occurs first, for—
>
> (A) wages, salaries, or commissions, including vacation, severance, and sick leave pay earned by an individual; or
>
> (B) sales commissions earned by an individual or by a corporation with only 1 employee, acting as an independent contractor in the sale of goods or services for the debtor in the ordinary course of the debtor's business if, and only if, during the 12 months preceding that date, at least 75 percent of the amount that the individual or corporation earned by acting as an independent contractor in the sale of goods or services was earned from the debtor.

(5) Fifth, allowed unsecured claims for contributions to an employee benefit plan—

(A) arising from services rendered within 180 days before the date of the filing of the petition or the date of the cessation of the debtor's business, whichever occurs first; but only

(B) for each such plan, to the extent of—

(i) the number of employees covered by each such plan multiplied by $10,000; less

(ii) the aggregate amount paid to such employees under paragraph (4) of this subsection, plus the aggregate amount paid by the estate on behalf of such employees to any other employee benefit plan.

[*11 U.S.C. §507(a)(4) and (5) (new text in italics)*]

Three significant changes were made to priorities. First the time period for the fourth priority of wages, salaries, or commissions, including vacation, severance, and sick leave pay earned by an individual, has been increased from 90 days to 180 days prior to bankruptcy. Second, the dollar limit has been increased from $4,925 to $10,000 for each individual. Third, the allowed cap on wages, salaries, and related expenses and unsecured claims for contributions to an employee benefit plan has also been increased to $10,000 from $4,925.

9.4 Eighth Priority: Defining Priority Tax Claims (2005 Act Section 705)

(a) Practice Prior to 2005 Act

Bankruptcy Code section 507(a)(8)(A)-(G) defines certain tax claims entitled to priority in payment. More importantly, a priority tax claim cannot be discharged in an individual's bankruptcy proceeding. [11 U.S.C. §523(a)] Every analysis of any unpaid tax liability requires an initial determination of whether the liability has "aged" or "matured" sufficiently to fall outside the time limitations defined in Code section 507(a)(8), thus clearing one hurdle toward being discharged.

Code section 507(a)(8) defines two "priority" time frames: 1) less than three years from the date that a return was due, as extended, until a petition was filed (three-year period) and 2) less than 240 days have passed after the tax was assessed (240-day period) until the voluntary petition was filed.

Under current law, if an offer-in-compromise is filed during the 240-day period, that time frame is extended by the amount of time the offer was pending plus 30 days.

Until the U.S. Supreme Court's decision in *Young*,[1] a question existed as to whether the three-year period or the 240-day period was tolled by the filing of a chapter 13 during the 3-year period or the 240-day period. In one fact pattern, chapter 13 petitions would be filed and dismissed and then refiled until the three-year period or the 240-day period had expired; then a chapter 7 would be filed. That chapter 7 filing was said to have discharged individual income tax liabilities.

The taxing authorities insisted that the filing of those bankruptcies (the chapter 13s) tolled the running of the three-year and the 240-day periods. Why? The automatic stay in effect during chapter 13 prohibited the taxing authority from collecting the tax. In *Young v. United States*, the U.S. Supreme Court finally agreed.

That is the law of the land and the current law. However, *Young* was decided after the new Bankruptcy Act was written, yet long before it had passed.

(b) Changes Enacted

Code section 507 (a)(8) as modified follows:

> (8) Eighth, allowed unsecured claims of governmental units, only to the extent that such claims are for—
>
> > (A) a tax on or measured by income or gross receipts *for a taxable year ending on or before the date of the filing of the petition*—
> >
> > > (i) for which a return, if required, is last due, including extensions, after three years before the date of the filing of the petition;
> > >
> > > (ii) assessed within 240 days *before the date of the filing of the petition, exclusive of*—
> > >
> > > > *(I)* anytime during which an offer in compromise with respect to *that tax* was pending, or *in effect during that 240-day period, plus 30 days; and*
> > > >
> > > > *(II) anytime during which a stay of proceedings against collections was in effect in a prior case under this title during that 240-day period, plus 90 days.*

---

[1] *Young v. United States*, 535 U.S. 43 (U.S. 2002).

(iii) other than a tax of a kind specified in section 523 (a)(1)(B) or 523 (a)(1)(C) of this title, not assessed before, but assessable, under applicable law or by agreement, after, the commencement of the case;

(B) a property tax *incurred* before the commencement of the case and last payable without penalty after one year before the date of the filing of the petition;

(C) a tax required to be collected or withheld and for which the debtor is liable in whatever capacity;

(D) an employment tax on a wage, salary, or commission of a kind specified in paragraph *(4)* of this subsection earned from the debtor before the date of the filing of the petition, whether or not actually paid before such date, for which a return is last due, under applicable law or under any extension, after three years before the date of the filing of the petition;

(E) an excise tax on—

(i) a transaction occurring before the date of the filing of the petition for which a return, if required, is last due, under applicable law or under any extension, after three years before the date of the filing of the petition; or

(ii) if a return is not required, a transaction occurring during the three years immediately preceding the date of the filing of the petition;

(F) a customs duty arising out of the importation of merchandise—

(i) entered for consumption within one year before the date of the filing of the petition;

(ii) covered by an entry liquidated or reliquidated within one year before the date of the filing of the petition; or

(iii) entered for consumption within four years before the date of the filing of the petition but unliquidated on such date, if the Secretary of the Treasury certifies that failure to liquidate such entry was due to an investigation pending on such date into assessment of antidumping or countervailing duties or fraud, or if information needed for the proper appraisement or classification of such merchandise was not available to the appropriate customs officer before such date; or

(G) a penalty related to a claim of a kind specified in this paragraph and in compensation for actual pecuniary loss.

An otherwise applicable time period specified in this paragraph shall be suspended for any period during which a governmental unit is prohibited under applicable nonbankruptcy law from collecting a tax as a result of a request by the debtor for a hearing and an appeal of any collection action taken or proposed against the debtor, plus 90 days; plus any time during which the stay of proceedings was in effect in a prior case under this title or during which collection was precluded by the existence of 1 or more confirmed plans under this title, plus 90 days.

[*11 U.S.C. §507(a)(8) (new text in italics)*]

While a lot of words were moved around, no truly substantive change emerges from the new word arrangement, with one exception. The 2005 Act rewrites the language dealing with 240-day period and offers-in-compromise—cosmetic but helpful changes.

In what appears to be a drafting anomaly, the 2005 Act adds an unnumbered and unlettered freestanding paragraph at the end of Code section 507(a)(8). Actually, this paragraph could not have been added as part of section 507(a)(8) without restructuring the entirety of Code section 507. The paragraph contains the language adopting the *Young* opinion and one new finite point dealing with the same concept as *Young*.

The new point deals with tolling the three-year and the 240-day periods for administrative tax processes. In some ways, the new language should be reviewed more closely for what it does and does not say. The language does expressly suspend the running of both priority time periods (what lawyers like to call "tolling") if the governmental unit is prohibited under applicable "nonbankruptcy" law from collecting the tax as a result of a request by a taxpayer for a hearing and an appeal of any collection action taken or proposed against the debtor. This language solely addresses the collection due-process hearings, and the right to judicial review of any determination made by the IRS at those hearings, under IRC sections 6320 and 6330.

What the amendment does not say is that tolling occurs if the taxing authority suspends collection action for any of a variety of other administrative reasons. The language is clear: "prohibited under applicable nonbankruptcy law." Not prohibited (as opposed to discretionary) or administrative decision (and not a statute or judicial decision) do not appear to satisfy the plain meaning of the Act's language.

(c) Impact of Changes

In summary, these amendments do not change existing law in any significant fashion. Perhaps more accurately, even if regarded as significant, the amendments were not unexpected and certainly not an extraordinary departure from what the private sector and the taxing authorities believed the law should have been under prior law.

Conceptually, taxes should be entitled to a priority distribution in the bankruptcy process, assuming the taxing authorities have not had a reasonable amount of time to collect the taxes. During that reasonable time period, the taxing authorities should collect the tax. When that time expires, the taxes are stale and no longer enjoy any preference in the bankruptcy distribution scheme. However that time should not run if the taxing authority is prevented by other legal process, the automatic stay in bankruptcy, or by statute, IRC section 6330, from collecting the tax. The amendments make that clear.

9.5 "Incurred" Property Taxes: A Fix in Language (2005 Act Section 706)

Existing Code section 507(a)(8)(B) defined property taxes entitled to a priority as being "assessed" prior to the filing of a voluntary petition. In many states and in local governments, the liability for property taxes arises at a given time by statute but is not "assessed" until sometime later. The term *assessed* is a term of art. Some statutes have it; others do not. Use of the term varies from state to state and has caused some legitimate concern due to its ambiguity as a determinant of priority for property taxes.

The term *incurred* as used in the 2005 Act focuses on when the tax debt arose, a fair and not terribly difficult event to identify. Thus, exactly when a property tax is "incurred" will be, according to some, easier to define than when it was "assessed." Time will tell.

9.6 New Tenth Priority: Driving Under the Influence (2005 Act Section 223)

A new tenth priority provides:

> *(10) Tenth, allowed claims for death or personal injury resulting from the operation of a motor vehicle or vessel if such operation was unlawful because the debtor was intoxicated from using alcohol, a drug, or another substance.*

[*11 U.S.C. §507(a)(10) (new text in italics)*]

Claims arising from personal injury or death due to an individual operating a vehicle or vessel while intoxicated from using alcohol or drugs will now be a priority claim.

9.7 Effective Date of Changes

The provisions of the 2005 Act generally are effective for cases filed on or after October 17, 2005. All of the provisions discussed above become effective for cases filed on or after October 17, 2005 except for the provision in 9.3 dealing with wages and employee benefits that is effective for petitions filed on or after April 20, 2005.

Chapter 10

New Chapter 15: Ancillary and Other Cross-Border Cases

The 2005 Act codifies significant changes with respect to the relief available to foreign debtors in the United States by creating a new chapter—Chapter 15, Ancillary and Other Cross-Border Cases (chapter 15).

10.1 Purpose/Interpretation

The purpose of chapter 15 is to "incorporate the Model Law on Cross-Border Insolvency so as to provide effective mechanisms for dealing with cases of cross-border insolvency." [11 U.S.C. §1501(a)] Specifically, the new statute is intended to accomplish several objectives, including:

- Promoting cooperation between (a) courts, trustees, United States trustees, examiners, debtors and debtors-in-possession in the United States and (b) courts and other "competent authorities of foreign countries in cross-border insolvency cases";
- Fostering "greater legal certainty for trade and investment";
- Providing guidancc designed to encourage "fair and efficient administration of cross-border insolvencies that protects the interests of all creditors, and other interested entities, including the debtor";
- Protecting and maximizing the value of the debtor's assets; and
- Facilitating the "rescue of financially troubled businesses, thereby protecting investment and preserving employment."

[11 U.S.C. §1501(a)(1)-(5)]

The promotion of cooperation between U.S. and foreign entities involved in cross-border insolvencies is not new to the Bankruptcy Code. Former Code section 304 (repealed by the 2005 Act) permitted foreign debtors to invoke U.S. bankruptcy laws in a limited way, the

---

 William H. Schrag and Wendy S. Walker acknowledge the contribution of Amanda R. Waller, an associate in the Finance and Restructuring Group of the New York office of Morgan, Lewis & Bockius LLP.

primary goal being to assist foreign proceedings, albeit while protecting U.S. creditors and assets.

New chapter 15 continues and reinforces this policy of cooperation by enunciating the foregoing objectives, as well as including other provisions, such as Code section 1508, which provides that, in interpreting chapter 15, courts "*shall* consider its international origin, and the need to promote an application of this chapter that is consistent with the application of similar statutes adopted by foreign jurisdictions." 11 U.S.C. §1508 (emphasis added).[1] In addition, subchapter IV of chapter 15 provides that bankruptcy courts and persons authorized by the courts in cross-border cases "*shall* cooperate to the maximum extent possible with a foreign court or a foreign representative." [11 U.S.C. §1525 (emphasis added)]

Furthermore, sections 1526 and 1527 set forth ways in which bankruptcy courts may cooperate with foreign courts, including the following:

1. Bankruptcy judges are authorized to appoint persons to act in cross-border cases and both they and the courts may communicate directly with and request information or assistance from foreign courts or representatives;
2. Sharing information;
3. "Coordination of the administration and supervision of debtor's assets and affairs";
4. "[A]pproval or implementation of agreements concerning the coordination of proceedings"; and
5. Coordination of concurrent proceedings.

As with the philosophy behind chapter 15, these approved forms of cooperation are not new. Rather, the designation of representatives, the use of protocols and direct communication between foreign and U.S. judges are practices that have evolved and are now accepted practices through their use in numerous cross-border cases. [*See, e.g., In re Board of Directors of Hopewell Int'l Ins. Ltd.*, 238 B.R. 25, 53-54 (Bankr. S.D.N.Y. 2002), *aff'd*, 275 B.R. 699 (S.D.N.Y. 2002) (appointing "duly selected" foreign representative over objection by creditor); *In re Maxwell Comm. Corp. plc*, 170 B.R. 800, 802 (Bankr. S.D.N.Y.

---

[1] The Model Law on Cross-border Insolvency, promulgated by the United Nations Commission on International Trade Law, has been adopted by the British Virgin Islands, Eritrea, Japan, Mexico, Montenegro, Poland, Romania, and South Africa. *Status 1997—Model Law on Cross-border Insolvency* (July 19, 2005), http://www.uncitral.org/uncitral/en/uncitral_texts/insolvency/1997 Model_status.html.

1994), *aff'd*, 186 B.R. 807 (S.D.N.Y. 1995) ("*Maxwell II*"), *aff'd*, 93 F.3d 1036 (2d Cir. 1996) ("*Maxwell III*") (establishing protocol to harmonize insolvency proceedings in the United Kingdom with chapter 11 proceedings in the United States).]

10.2 Who May Be a Debtor Under Chapter 15

Having been given no guidance under the previously existing provisions of the Code, courts have generally held that the requirements of Code section 109 regarding eligibility to be a debtor were inapplicable to ancillary cases involving foreign debtors. [*See, e.g., In re Goerg*, 844 F.2d 1562, 1568 (11th Cir. 1988), *cert. denied sub nom, Parungao v. Goerg*, 488 U.S. 1034 (1989); *In re Saleh*, 175 B.R. 422, 425 (Bankr. S.D. Fla. 1994); *In re Brierley*, 145 B.R. 151, 159 (Bankr. S.D.N.Y. 1992).] Chapter 15 clarifies this issue and sets out specifically the types of entities and proceedings to which it does, and does not, apply. Pursuant to Code section 1501(b), chapter 15 applies to (1) a foreign court or representative seeking assistance in the United States in connection with a foreign proceeding, (2) an entity seeking assistance in a foreign country with respect to a case under Title 11, (3) concurrently pending foreign and U.S. Title 11 cases and (4) interested parties in a foreign country who wish to commence or participate in a Title 11 case. [11 U.S.C. §1501(b)] Chapter 15 expressly does not apply to, among others, entities prohibited from being debtors pursuant to amended Code section 109(b).[2]

10.3 Venue

Whereas the prior statute contained requirements with respect to the venue of an ancillary proceeding based on the relief sought pursuant to 28 U.S.C. §1410 (as amended by the Act), a case under chapter 15 may be commenced in the district where the foreign debtor's principal assets or principal place of business in the United States are located, or, if none, in the district where an action in state or federal

---

[2] This includes foreign banks, savings banks, cooperative banks, savings and loan associations, building and loan associations and credit unions that have a branch or agency (as defined in §1(b) of the International Banking Act of 1978) in the United States. This provision thus effectively overrules the district court's decision *In re Agency for Deposit Insurance, Rehabilitation, Bankruptcy and Liquidation of Banks v. Superintendent of Banks of the State of New York*, 310 B.R. 793 (S.D.N.Y. 2004), *appeal docketed*, Nos. 04-4997, 04-4999 (2d Cir. Sept. 17, 2004), holding that the exclusion of foreign banks from eligibility to be a debtor under Code section 109 is irrelevant to the analysis of whether an entity is qualified to commence an ancillary case under section 304. *Id.* Pursuant to amended Code section 109, foreign insurance companies engaged in such business in the United States are similarly ineligible to be debtors and are thus ineligible to be debtors under chapter 15. 11 U.S.C. §109(b)(3)(A).

court is pending against the foreign debtor, or, if there are no assets, business or pending actions, in the district "in which venue will be consistent with the interests of justice and the convenience of the parties, having regard to the relief sought by the foreign representative." [28 U.S.C. §1410(3)]

10.4 Commencement of a Case Under Chapter 15

A case is commenced under sections 1504 and 1515 by the filing with the bankruptcy court by a foreign representative[3] of a petition for "recognition" of a foreign proceeding.[4] The recognition petition must be accompanied by evidence of the commencement of a foreign proceeding and of the appointment of the foreign representative and a statement identifying all of the pending foreign proceedings. [11 U.S.C. §1515]. To the extent that such documents are issued by a foreign entity, they need not be supported by authenticating affidavits; rather, the court is permitted to presume their authenticity. [11 U.S.C. §1516]. The recognition petition will be granted if the forego-

---

[3] The definition of the term *foreign representative* has been changed to mean "a person or body, including a person or body appointed on an interim basis, authorized in a foreign proceeding *to administer the reorganization or the liquidation of the debtor's assets* or affairs or to act as a representative of such foreign proceeding." (11 U.S.C. §101(24) (as amended) (emphasis added). *Cf. In re Goerg*, 844 F2d 1562 (11th Cir. 1988), *cert denied sub nom, Parungao v. Goerg*, 488 U.S. 1034 (1989) (holding that foreign representative of foreign insolvent decedent's estate was qualified to commence ancillary proceeding under section 304, even though a decedent's estate would not qualify as a "debtor" under section 109). Section 1502 contains the following new definitions: (1) recognition "means the entry of an order granting recognition of a foreign main proceeding or a foreign nonmain proceeding under this chapter"; (2) foreign main proceeding "means a foreign proceeding pending in the country where the debtor has the center of its main interests" (pursuant to section 1516(c), a debtor's registered office is presumed to be the center of its main interests; however, the presumption is rebuttable and is therefore an area ripe for litigation); (3) foreign nonmain proceeding "means a foreign proceeding, other than a foreign main proceeding, pending in a country where the debtor has an establishment" and (4) establishment "means any place of operations where the debtor carries out a nontransitory economic activity." In addition, the definition of "foreign proceeding" has been amended to mean "a collective judicial or administrative proceeding in a foreign country, including an interim proceeding, under a law relating to insolvency or adjustment of debt in which proceeding the assets and affairs of the debtor are subject to control or supervision by a foreign court for the purpose of reorganization or liquidation." 11 U.S.C. §101(23) (as amended). Thus, the Bankruptcy Code recognizes ancillary as well as plenary foreign proceedings. In addition, in contrast to the Model Law, the commencement of a plenary case outside the U.S. does not preclude a foreign debtor from seeking plenary relief in the United States.

ing requirements are met and the foreign proceeding meets the definition of a *foreign main proceeding* or a *foreign nonmain proceeding*.[5]

The court must make a determination with respect to the petition for recognition "at the earliest possible time" and may modify or terminate such determination upon a change of circumstances, giving "due weight to possible prejudice to parties that have relied upon the order granting recognition." [11 U.S.C. §1517(c) and (d)]. Pursuant to section 1518, a foreign representative is obligated to file a notice with the court of any "substantial change" in the status of the foreign proceeding or the foreign representative and of any additional foreign proceedings. The court has an obligation following subsequent filings to coordinate the relief granted in such proceedings so as to be consistent with each other and with any pending foreign main proceeding.

Thus, as with the previously existing system under Code section 304, prerequisites for the commencement of an ancillary proceeding are minimal and, although the automatic stay does not apply upon the *filing* of the petition (as distinguished from its new applicability, discussed below, upon the *recognition* of a foreign main proceeding), a request for provisional relief may be filed with the petition. [*See, e.g., In re Manning*, 236 B.R. 14, 20 (B.A.P. 9th Cir. 1999) (the debtor's ownership of property in the United States is not the "sine qua non" of subject matter jurisdiction under section 304); *Hopewell*, 238 B.R. at 49-51 (broadly construing the term "foreign proceeding"); *In re Evans*, 177 B.R. 193, 196-97 (Bankr. S.D.N.Y. 1995) (allowing turnover proceeding commenced by foreign representative under section 304).]

10.5 Relief Available Between Petition Filing and Recognition of Foreign Proceeding

While the provisional relief typically requested on the first day of a case under section 304 could be very broad and would remain in place, subject to periodic review, throughout the life of the ancillary proceeding, under chapter 15, relief granted in conjunction with the filing of the petition is limited to that which is "urgently needed" and terminates (without prejudice) once the petition is granted. Thereafter, the foreign representative will likely seek post-recognition relief. [*See* 11 U.S.C. §1507].

Upon the filing of the petition for recognition but prior to the court's determination of whether the petition should be granted, the foreign representative may seek and the court may grant provisional relief "urgently needed to protect the debtor's assets or the interests

---

[5] The filing of a recognition petition does not subject the foreign representative to the jurisdiction of any U.S. court for any other purpose. 11 U.S.C. §1510.

of creditors," including (i) a stay of execution against the debtor's assets; (ii) turnover of the responsibility for administering or realizing on assets of the debtor in the U.S. to the foreign representative or other person authorized by the court for the purpose of protecting and preserving perishable, devaluing or otherwise jeopardized assets;[6] (iii) freezing the debtor's assets; (iv) discovery and (v) other relief available to a trustee (except for relief available under sections 522, 544, 545, 547, 548, 550 and 724(a)). [11 U.S.C. §1519(a)].[7]

10.6 Effect of Recognition

Upon the grant by a court of a petition for recognition, (1) "a court in the United States *shall* grant comity or cooperation to the foreign representative;" (2) a foreign representative may, in the case of a foreign main proceeding, commence a voluntary or involuntary case under sections 301, 302 or 303;[8] (3) the foreign representative automatically becomes a party in interest in any case pending against the debtor under Title 11; (4) the foreign representative may sue and be sued in the United States; (5) the foreign representative may "apply directly to a court in the United States for appropriate relief;" and (6) the foreign representative may intervene in any proceeding in state or federal court where the debtor is a party. [11 U.S.C. §§1509, 1511, 1512, 1524 (emphasis added)].[9]

In addition, in a change that is important to U.S. creditors of foreign debtors, pursuant to section 1520, upon the recognition of a foreign main proceeding, (1) Code sections 361 (adequate protection) and 362 (automatic stay) apply with respect to any property of the debtor located in the United States.; (2) section 363 (sale or use of property), section 549 (postpetition transfers) and section 552 (liens on after-

---

[6] Code section 1104(d) (appointment of disinterested person as trustee or examiner) applies in chapter 15. 11 U.S.C. §1522 (d).

[7] The standard for a grant of relief under section 1519 is an injunction standard. 11 U.S.C. §1519(e). Such relief must be denied where it would interfere with a foreign main proceeding and terminates when the recognition petition is granted. 11 U.S.C. §1519 (b) and (c). The relief under this section cannot be used to enjoin a police or regulatory act of a governmental unit or to stay rights not subject to the automatic stay under sections 362(b)(6), (7), (17) or (27) or 362(n). 11 U.S.C. §§1519 (d) and (f).

[8] Recognition of a foreign main proceeding constitutes proof that the debtor is insolvent for purposes of section 303. 11 U.S.C. §1531. A voluntary case may only be commenced by the foreign representative if the foreign proceeding is a foreign main proceeding. 11 U.S.C. §1511 (a)(2).

[9] Irrespective of whether recognition is granted, a foreign representative is always subject to applicable nonbankruptcy law. Irrespective of whether a foreign representative seeks recognition, a foreign representative may exercise any available right to collect or recover a claim that is property of the debtor. 11 U.S.C. §1509 (e) and (f).

acquired property) apply to transfers of property of the debtor in the United States; (3) the foreign representative is empowered to operate the debtor and take action under sections 363 and 552 and (4) section 552 applies to property of the debtor in the U.S.[10]

U.S. creditors of foreign debtors should be particularly mindful of these provisions given the consequences of violating the automatic stay, which may include sanctions and contempt orders for repeated violations. The application of Code sections 361, 363, 549 and 552 to foreign debtors, however, should provide significant protections to U.S. creditors in that the use or sale of a debtor's property located in the U.S. will be subject to the protection of the interests of creditors with interests in such property.

10.7 Additional Relief Available Post-Recognition

Pursuant to Code section 1507, if recognition is granted the foreign representative may seek "additional assistance" from the bankruptcy court. In determining whether to provide such assistance, the bankruptcy court must "consider whether such additional assistance, consistent with principles of comity," is also consistent with the principles listed in former Code section 304, including just treatment of holders of claims, protection of U.S. creditors from prejudice and inconvenience of prosecuting claims in a foreign proceeding, preventing fraudulent and preferential transfers, distribution of proceeds substantially in accordance with the Bankruptcy Code's priorities and an opportunity for a fresh start. In addition, a court may always refuse to act if to do so would be "manifestly contrary" to U.S. public policy. [11 U.S.C. §1506]

It is also important to note that relief under either section 1519 (relief available postfiling, but prerecognition) or section 1520 (Code provisions applicable upon recognition of foreign main proceeding) may be (1) granted, modified or terminated *sua sponte* upon the request of the foreign representative or an affected entity "only if the interests of the creditors and other interested entities, including the debtor, are sufficiently protected" or (2) subjected to conditions, including the posting of a bond or other security. [11 U.S.C. §1522(a) and (b)]

More specifically, upon the recognition of a foreign proceeding, main or nonmain, "where necessary to effectuate the purpose of this chapter and to protect the assets of the debtor or the interests of

---

[10] This section does not prevent the commencement of an action in a foreign country to preserve a claim against the debtor or the ability of a foreign representative to commence a case under Title 11 or the right of other parties in interest to file claims and take permitted actions in such a case. 11 U.S.C. §1520(b) and (c).

creditors," the foreign representative may request and the court may grant additional relief, including (1) a stay of any action or proceeding; (2) a stay of execution against the debtor's assets; (3) suspension of the right to transfer, encumber or dispose of any assets; (4) discovery; (5) turnover of the administration or realization of the debtor's assets to the foreign representative or other authorized person; (6) the extension of any relief previously granted under section 1519 during the interim period between the filing and granting of the recognition petition; (7) other relief available to a trustee (other than under Code sections 522, 544, 545, 547, 548, 550 and 724(a)) and (8) authorization to distribute the debtor's assets located in the United States, which may be granted only if "the court is satisfied that the interests of creditors in the United States are sufficiently protected." [11 U.S.C. §1521(a) and (b)].[11]

10.8 Concurrent Plenary Cases

Concurrent plenary cases, previously unmentioned in the Bankruptcy Code, are now the subject of subchapter V of chapter 15. Section 1528 provides that following recognition of a foreign main proceeding, a case under another chapter of Title 11 may be commenced only if the debtor has assets in the United States.[12] Section 1528 further provides:

---

[11] In granting relief under section 1521 with respect to a foreign nonmain proceeding, the court must be "satisfied that the relief relates to assets that, under the law of the United States, should be administered in the foreign nonmain proceeding or concerns information required in that proceeding." 11 U.S.C. §1521(c). The standard for a grant of relief under section 1521 is an injunction standard. 11 U.S.C. §1521 (e). The relief under this section (as under section 1519) cannot be used to enjoin a police or regulatory act of a governmental unit or to stay rights not subject to the automatic stay under section 362 (b)(6), (7), (17) or (27) or section 362 (n). 11 U.S.C. §1521 (d) and (f).

[12] Section 1528 does not distinguish between voluntary plenary cases under Bankruptcy Code §301 and involuntary plenary cases under section 303 (b)(4), each of which may be commenced by a foreign representative in accordance with 11 U.S.C. §1528 and so long as the other eligibility requirements are met. *Cf,* 11 U.S.C. §1511. Furthermore, under current section 305, a plenary case may be dismissed or the court may abstain from hearing the case if, among other things, there is a foreign proceeding pending or based on the factors set forth in section 304. *See In re Globo Comuncacoes E Participacoes S.A.*, 317 B.R. 235 (S.D.N.Y. 2004) (bankruptcy court dismissal of involuntary case filed against debtor in foreign proceeding vacated and remanded by district court, with instructions to make specific findings whether, among other things, abstention warranted under section 305 based upon factors listed in section 304 (c)). Section 305 has been amended by the 2005 Act to provide that a case may be dismissed or a court may abstain if a recognition petition has been granted or if the purposes of chapter 15 would be best served.

> The effects of such case shall be restricted to the assets of the debtor that are within the territorial jurisdiction of the United States and, to the extent necessary to implement cooperation and coordination under sections 1525, 1526 and 1527, to other assets of the debtor that are within the jurisdiction of the court under section 541(a) of this title and section 1334(e) of title 28, to the extent that such other assets are not subject to the jurisdiction and control of a foreign proceeding that has been recognized under this chapter.[13]

In concurrent cross-border insolvency proceedings under the prior version of the Code, U.S. courts had no restrictions on their exercise of jurisdiction over the debtor's statutory property. The new limitations imposed by chapter 15, designed to further its goals of cooperation and coordination, may limit the discretion and power of U.S. courts in concurrent cross-border cases.[14]

Subchapter V further provides that (1) to the extent that a concurrent plenary case is filed, relief granted under section 1519 or 1521 must be consistent (or modified so as to be consistent) with such plenary case and section 1520 (regarding the applicability of the automatic stay and other sections) no longer applies; and (2) to the extent that a foreign nonmain case is filed, the court must ensure that any relief granted relates to assets that, under U.S. law, should be administered in the foreign nonmain proceeding. [11 U.S.C. §1529] In a concurrent plenary case commenced in the U.S., the court may also authorize a person or entity to act in the foreign proceeding and such person may act in any way permitted by foreign law. [11 U.S.C. §1505]

10.9 Avoidance Actions Under Chapter 15

Although the foreign representative is not authorized to pursue avoidance actions under Code sections 522, 544, 545, 547, 548, 550 or 724(a) in an ancillary proceeding under chapter 15, the foreign representative may do so in any case involving the debtor under another chapter of Title 11 so long as, in the case of a foreign nonmain pro-

---

13 Section 541(a) provides that the commencement of a case creates an estate comprising all property of the debtor "wherever located and by whomever held." 11 U.S.C. §541 (a). Pursuant to 28 U.S.C. §1334 (e), the district court in which a case is commenced has exclusive jurisdiction over all such property.

14 Although there are no statutory restrictions, practical limitations may exist. *See In re Yukos Oil Co.*, 321 B.R. 396, 410-11 (Bankr. S.D. Tex. 2005) (dismissing case based on inability to grant relief due to lack of participation of Russian government, questionable exercise of U.S. jurisdiction and proceedings pending in other countries).

ceeding, the court is satisfied that such an action relates to assets which, under U.S. law, should be administered in the foreign non-main proceeding. [11 U.S.C. §1523].

As set forth above, after recognition of a foreign main proceeding a foreign representative may only commence a plenary action in the United States if the debtor has assets in the United States and the U.S. court's jurisdiction only reaches those assets and other assets not within the jurisdiction of the foreign court. [11 U.S.C. §1528] Thus, chapter 15 states clearly that avoidance actions are available to foreign debtors; and it resolves the choice of law issue that arises when U.S. and foreign plenary proceedings are commenced and avoidance actions exist. This is consistent with more recent case law on these issues. [*See, e.g., Maxwell III*, 93 F.3d at 1051-52; *cf. In re Axona Int'l Credit & Commerce Ltd.*, 88 B.R. 597, 613-615.]

10.10 Rights of Foreign Creditors in U.S. Cases

Foreign creditors, heretofore unmentioned in the Bankruptcy Code, now have recognized rights under sections 1513 and 1514. These rights include the following: (1) "the same rights regarding the commencement of, and participation in, a case under this title as domestic creditors"; (2) foreign creditors with priority claims under sections 507 or 726 "shall not be given a lower priority than that of general unsecured claims without priority solely because the holder of such claim is a foreign creditor"; (3) any notice that must be given to creditors generally must also be given to foreign creditors; (4) such notice must be individual notice unless the court otherwise directs; (5) notice of the commencement of the case must give information regarding the mechanism and timing for filing proofs of claim and (6) a reasonable amount of additional time to file proofs of claim must be provided to foreign creditors.

10.11 Conclusion

Although much of chapter 15 represents the codification of standards and practices which have evolved through case law under former Code section 304, there are certain important new changes, including (1) the applicability of the automatic stay and other provisions with respect to cases commenced in the U.S. which are ancillary to foreign main proceedings; (2) the limitations on the extent of jurisdiction of U.S. courts in concurrent plenary cases and (3) the recognition of the rights of foreign creditors.

10.12 Effective Date of Changes

As with most of the changes made by the 2005 Act, new chapter 15 is effective with respect to cases commenced on or after October 17, 2005.

Chapter 11

Consumer Issues: Means Testing

11.1 Introduction

One of the key reasons for the revisions to the Bankruptcy Code was to prevent perceived abuses in consumer bankruptcies. An important part of the basis for reducing consumer abuses was the establishment of means testing provisions. Under the means test, a debtor having income above the state median may, rather than receiving a discharge of all debts, be required to make payments to creditors from future earnings. Other provisions affecting consumers, including the changes to chapter 13, are discussed in Chapter 12 of this publication.

11.2 Practice Prior to 2005 Act

Before the Bankruptcy Abuse Prevention and Consumer Protection Act of 2005 (2005 Act), an individual could file a chapter 7 petition; use the available assets other than exempt assets, if any, to pay first priority claims; and, if any funds were left, make a partial payment of unsecured claims and have the balance of its debt discharged. Code section 707(b) provided that "after notice and a hearing, the court, on its own motion or on a motion by the United States trustee, but not at the request or suggestion of any party in interest, may dismiss a case filed by an individual debtor under this chapter whose debts are primarily consumer debts if it finds that the granting of relief would be a substantial abuse of the provisions of this chapter." The Code also provided that "[t]here shall be a presumption in favor of granting the relief requested by the debtor." This provision, according to some creditors, especially credit card companies, did not prevent the abuses these companies and others believed existed.

11.3 Changes Enacted (2005 Act Section 102)

(a) General Provision for Abuse

If a case involving primarily the consumer debts of an individual debtor is determined to be an abuse of Bankruptcy Code provisions, chapter 7 may not be an available alternative. As amended, Code section 707(b)(1) now provides the following:

> (b)(1) After notice and a hearing, the court, on its own motion or on a motion by the United States trustee, *trustee (or bankruptcy administrator, if any), or* any

> party in interest, may dismiss a case filed by an individual debtor under this chapter whose debts are primarily consumer debts, *or, with the debtor's consent, convert such a case to a case under chapter 11 or 13 of this title,* if it finds that the granting of relief would be *an* abuse of the provisions of this chapter. In making a determination whether to dismiss a case under this section, the court may not take into consideration whether a debtor has made, or continues to make, charitable contributions (that meet the definition of "charitable contribution" under section 548(d)(3)) to any qualified religious or charitable entity or organization (as that term is defined in section 548(d)(4)).

[*11 U.S.C. §707(b)(1) (new text in italics)*]

The revisions to the Code specifically provide that any party in interest, including a trustee or the U.S. trustee, may file a motion with the court to dismiss the case. Prior to the 2005 Act, this section provided that a party in interest could not file a motion. In line with the effort to see that more chapter 7 consumer cases are dismissed or converted primarily to chapter 13, the provision that "[t]here shall be a presumption in favor of granting the relief requested by the debtor" was removed from the statute.

(b) Income Less Than State Median

If the annual income determined by multiplying the current monthly income by 12 is less than the median family income, it will be presumed that an abuse does not exist. No party, including the bankruptcy judge and the U.S. trustee, can file a motion claiming an abuse based on the income of the debtor. However, see section 11.5 below for other bases for the bankruptcy judge or U.S. trustee to file a motion for abuse.

New Code section 707(b)(7) provides that an abuse will not be presumed unless the annual income of the debtor is greater than the state median income:

> *(7) (A) No judge, United States trustee (or bankruptcy administrator, if any), trustee, or other party in interest may file a motion under paragraph (2) if the current monthly income of the debtor, including a veteran (as that term is defined in section 101 of title 38), and the debtor's spouse combined, as of the date of the order for relief, when multiplied by 12, is equal to or less than—*

(i) in the case of a debtor in a household of 1 person, the median family income of the applicable State for 1 earner;

(ii) in the case of a debtor in a household of 2, 3, or 4 individuals, the highest median family income of the applicable State for a family of the same number or fewer individuals; or

(iii) in the case of a debtor in a household exceeding 4 individuals, the highest median family income of the applicable State for a family of 4 or fewer individuals, plus $525 per month for each individual in excess of 4.

(B) In a case that is not a joint case, current monthly income of the debtor's spouse shall not be considered for the purposes of subparagraph (A) if—

(i) (I) the debtor and the debtor's spouse are separated under applicable nonbankruptcy law; or

(II) the debtor and the debtor's spouse are living separate and apart, other than for the purpose of evading subparagraph (A); and

(ii) the debtor files a statement under penalty of perjury—

(I) specifying that the debtor meets the requirement of subclause (I) or (II) of clause (i); and

(II) disclosing the aggregate, or best estimate of the aggregate, amount of any cash or money payment received from the debtor's spouse attributed to the debtor's current monthly income.

[*11 U.S.C. 707(b)(7) (new text in italics)*]

The median family income is, as defined in Code section 101(39A), the median family income both calculated and reported by the Bureau of the Census in the then most recent year. If not calculated and reported in the current year, the amount reported in the most recent year is adjusted annually after such most recent year until the next year in which median family income is both calculated and reported by the Bureau of the Census, to reflect the percentage change in the

Consumer Price Index for All Urban Consumers. If the size of the household is in excess of four, the median family income is increased by $525 per month for each member of the household in excess of four.

Median income is available at http://www.usdoj.gov/ust/ or from the clerk of the bankruptcy court. For example, in Oregon and New York the median family income to be used until the data is adjusted in early 2006 for various family sizes is listed as:

Household Size	***Oregon***	***New York***
1 person	$36,299	$39,463
2 person	47,080	48,492
3 person	52,842	57,430
4 person	58,986	67,564

In some states, the spread between the lowest and highest median incomes for one-person households was over $24,000: In Mississippi, the median income for a one-person household was only $28,288, while in New Jersey it was $52,000. For a four-person household, one of the largest income levels was Maryland at $85,554, while the lowest was New Mexico at $47,256.

Current monthly income is income from all sources that the debtor receives without regard to whether such income is taxable. It includes amounts received on a regular basis for the debtor's household expenses, including expense of the debtor's dependents, but excludes Social Security payments and selected payments to victims of war crimes or terrorism.

The current monthly income of the debtor is defined in Code section 101(10A):

> *(10A) The term "current monthly income"—*
>
> > *(A) means the average monthly income from all sources that the debtor receives (or in a joint case the debtor and the debtor's spouse receive) without regard to whether such income is taxable income, derived during the 6-month period ending on—*
> >
> > > *(i) the last day of the calendar month immediately preceding the date of the commencement of the case if the debtor files the schedule of current income required by section 521(a)(1)(B)(ii); or*
> > >
> > > *(ii) the date on which current income is determined by the court for purposes of*

this title if the debtor does not file the schedule of current income required by section 521(a)(1)(B)(ii); and

(B) includes any amount paid by any entity other than the debtor (or in a joint case the debtor and the debtor's spouse), on a regular basis for the household expenses of the debtor or the debtor's dependents (and in a joint case the debtor's spouse if not otherwise a dependent), but excludes benefits received under the Social Security Act, payments to victims of war crimes or crimes against humanity on account of their status as victims of such crimes, and payments to victims of international terrorism (as defined in section 2331 of title 18) or domestic terrorism (as defined in section 2331 of title 18) on account of their status as victims of such terrorism.

[*11 U.S.C §101(10A) (new text in italics)*]

As previously noted in Code section 707(b)(7)(A), "income" includes income earned by the debtor and the debtor's spouse unless they are separated; then the amount of the spouse's income received by the debtor would be included. If the debtor files the schedule of current income required under Code section 521, the monthly income will be based on the average monthly income for the six months ending just before the month in which the petition was filed. If the statement of monthly income was not filed, it will be based on the six months ending on the date determined by the bankruptcy court. By properly filing the schedule of income the debtor has some control over the period in which the average monthly income will be determined.

Interim Rules and Forms have been issued and are available at http://www.uscourts.gov/rules/interim.html or http://www.airacira.org/bankruptcy rules and forms/.

Example A

If the husband in a five-member household filed a chapter 7 petition on November 1, 2005, in Oregon, the median family income would be determined as follows:

Median household income for four, for 2005	$59,490
One additional household member at $525 per month	6,300
Total median household income	$65,790

Household income consists of the following for the six months prior to November, 2005, the month of petition filing:

Income earned by debtor	$16,000
Income earned by spouse	10,000
Funds received April 25, 2005, from debtor's parents (college tuition for one of the dependents)	10,000
Total	$36,000
Divided by six months	6
Average monthly income	$6,000
Multiplied by 12 months	12
Annual household income	$72,000

Under the above conditions, the debtor failed to satisfy the means test because the annual income of $72,000 was in excess of the median household income of $65,502. Whether the debtor will have the petition dismissed or converted to chapter 13 will depend on the analysis below.

Note that if the debtor's petition had been filed in the month of September, the funds received for college tuition for one of the dependents would not have been included in the past six months of income, resulting in the annual household income being less than the median household income of $65,502. Thus the debtor would have satisfied the means test and would have been allowed to remain in chapter 7 without further analysis.

(c) Income Greater Than State Median

In considering whether the granting of relief would be an abuse of the provisions of this chapter in situations where the average income is greater than the median state income, the court shall presume abuse exists if the debtor's current monthly income (average of the previous six months) reduced by the average monthly deduction listed below and multiplied by 60 is not less than the lesser of the following:

1. 25 percent of the debtor's nonpriority unsecured claims in the case, or $6,000, whichever is greater; or
2. $10,000.

Thus, if the debtor's current monthly income (average of the previous six months) reduced by the average monthly deduction listed below (monthly net income) exceeds $166.66 ($10,000 divided by 60), it will be presumed that abuse exists. If the monthly net income is less than $100 ($6,000 divided by 60), the presumption of abuse does not exist. If the net income is between $100 and $166.66, abuse exists if the net income is greater than 25 percent of the debtor's nonpriority unsecured claims. Under these conditions, abuse is presumed if the monthly net income is large enough to pay at least 25 percent of the nonpriority unsecured claims. For example, if the monthly net income is $100, abuse would not exist if the unsecured debt is greater than $24,000 (60 times 100, or $6,000, is less than 25 percent of $24,000.01). For instance, if the debtor's debt is $23,000, incurring additional debt in an amount in excess of $1,000 prior to filing the petition for a valid need and use may avoid the presumption of abuse. If the monthly net income is $166.66, the presumption of abuse does not exist if the nonpriority unsecured debt exceeds $39,998.40 ($166.66 times 60 divided by 25 percent).

Code section 707(b)(2)(A)(i) provides the following:

> *(i) In considering under paragraph (1) whether the granting of relief would be an abuse of the provisions of this chapter, the court shall presume abuse exists if the debtor's current monthly income reduced by the amounts determined under clauses (ii), (iii), and (iv), and multiplied by 60 is not less than the lesser of—*
>
> > *(I) 25 percent of the debtor's nonpriority unsecured claims in the case, or $6,000, whichever is greater; or*
> >
> > *(II) $10,000.*

[*11 U.S.C. §707(b)(2)(A)(ii), (iii), and (iv) (new text in italics)*]

(d) Deductions

Section 707(b)(2)(A) describes the deductions that are allowed in determining if an abuse exists. Information regarding the deduction is available at http://www.irs.gov, http://www.usdoj.gov/ust/, or from the clerk of the bankruptcy court. Deductions include:

1. *IRS guidelines.* The monthly expenses as defined in Code section 707(b)(2)(A)(ii), including deductions allowed as living expenses specified under standards of the IRS, are allowed to be used by the debtor. The IRS guidelines include:
   - *National Standards*—Allowances for food, clothing, and other items. Allowances are nationwide except for Alaska and Hawaii, which have separate allowances. It appears that the national standards apply, regardless of the amount actually spent.
   - *Local Standards*—Allowances for housing and utilities and transportation, known as the Local Standards, vary by location. The allowances for housing and utili-

ties are based on counties within the state and are divided into three levels—families of two or less, families of three, and families of four or more. Secured debt payments should not be included to the extent they are accounted for in the IRS Housing and Utility Standards.

— *Transportation Costs*—Transportation schedules are based on both national and regional standards. The national rate for 2005 is an allowance of $475 per month for ownership costs for the first vehicle and $338 for the second. The allowance for the first vehicle is reduced by the monthly secured debt payments related to that vehicle. The amount should not be reduced below zero. A similar reduction applies to a second vehicle. Operating and public transportation costs are for no car and one or two cars and are based on census regions and metropolitan statistical areas. If the taxpayer lives within one of the areas defined by city and county, the rate for that area would apply; if the taxpayer does not reside in one of these areas, the regional standard is used. For example, one of the metropolitan areas is Portland, consisting of the city of Portland, seven counties in Oregon and one county in Washington. All other counties in Oregon would use the regional rates.

2. *Expenses Not Specified by IRS.* Section 707(b)(2)(A)(ii), paragraph (I), of the 2005 Act provides that certain categories of expenses not specified by the IRS may also be allowed:

   — Reasonably necessary health insurance, disability insurance, and health savings account expenses for the debtor, the spouse of the debtor, or the dependents of the debtor.

   — Debtor's reasonably necessary expenses incurred to maintain the safety of the debtor and the family of the debtor from family violence.

   — An additional allowance for food and clothing of up to 5 percent of the food and clothing categories as specified by the National Standards issued by the IRS, provided it is shown that such costs are reasonable and necessary.

   — However, notwithstanding any other provision, the monthly expenses of the debtor shall not include payments for debts.

Unlike the National Standards for federal tax purposes, under Local Standards the taxpayer is allowed the amount actually spent *or* the standard, whichever is less. Based on the Code section 707(b)(2), "[D]ebtor's monthly expenses shall be the debtor's applicable monthly expense amounts specified under the National Standards and Local Standards." Furthermore, Code section 707 (b)(2)(A)(ii)(V) notes that "[i]n addition, the debtor's monthly expenses may include an allowance for housing and utilities, in excess of the allowance specified by the Local Standards for housing and utilities issued by the Internal Revenue Service, based on the actual expenses for home energy costs if the debtor provides documentation of such actual expenses and demonstrates that such actual expenses are reasonable and necessary." Payments on secured debt, such as mortgage payments, should not be included in the allowance to the extent they are accounted for in the IRS Housing and Utilities Standards.

3. *Expenses for Care of Family Member.* These include expenses paid by the debtor that are reasonable and necessary for care and support of an elderly, chronically ill, or disabled household member or member of the debtor's immediate family and who is unable to pay for such reasonable and necessary expenses.
4. *Chapter 13 Monthly Expenses.* These include expenses of the debtor to administer a chapter 13 plan for the district in which the debtor resides, up to 10 percent of the projected plan payments, as determined by the Executive Office of the U.S. Trustee.
5. *Special Educational Expenses.* These include the actual expenses for each dependent child less than 18 years of age (not to exceed $1,500 per year per child) to attend a private or public, elementary, or secondary school
6. *Excess Housing and Utilities.* This is an allowance for housing and utilities expense in excess of the allowance for these expenses in the Local Standards issued by the IRS; it is to be based on the actual expenses for home energy costs provided the debtor submits documentation of the actual expenses and demonstrates that the expenses are reasonable and necessary.
7. *Secured Debt Payments.* These are total secured debt due over the five years of the chapter 13 plan divided by 60 months; past-due secured payments included in the plan that are necessary for the debtor's possession of the pri-

mary residence, motor vehicle, or other property necessary for the support of the debtor and the debtor's dependents, are also considered.

8. *Priority Claims.* Debtor's expenses for payment of all priority claims (including priority child support and alimony claims) shall be calculated as the total amount of debts entitled to priority, divided by 60.
9. *Contributions.* Furthermore, Code section 707(b)(1) implies that the chapter 13 practice of allowing plan contributions to a tax-exempt charity is to be continued under the 2005 Act.

The text of Code section 707(b)(2)(A) (ii), (iii), and(iv) as added by the 2005 Act follows:

> *(ii) (I) The debtor's monthly expenses shall be the debtor's applicable monthly expense amounts specified under the National Standards and Local Standards, and the debtor's actual monthly expenses for the categories specified as Other Necessary Expenses issued by the Internal Revenue Service for the area in which the debtor resides, as in effect on the date of the order for relief, for the debtor, the dependents of the debtor, and the spouse of the debtor in a joint case, if the spouse is not otherwise a dependent. Such expenses shall include reasonably necessary health insurance, disability insurance, and health savings account expenses for the debtor, the spouse of the debtor, or the dependents of the debtor. Notwithstanding any other provision of this clause, the monthly expenses of the debtor shall not include any payments for debts. In addition, the debtor's monthly expenses shall include the debtor's reasonably necessary expenses incurred to maintain the safety of the debtor and the family of the debtor from family violence as identified under section 309 of the Family Violence Prevention and Services Act, or other applicable Federal law. The expenses included in the debtor's monthly expenses described in the preceding sentence shall be kept confidential by the court. In addition, if it is demonstrated that it is reasonably and necessary, the debtor's monthly expenses may also include an additional allowance for food and clothing of up to 5 percent of the food and clothing categories as specified by the National Standards issued by the Internal Revenue Service.*

(II) In addition, the debtor's monthly expenses may include, if applicable, the continuation of actual expenses paid by the debtor that are reasonable and necessary for care and support of an elderly, chronically ill, or disabled household member or member of the debtor's immediate family (including parents, grandparents, siblings, children, and grandchildren of the debtor, the dependents of the debtor, and the spouse of the debtor in a joint case who is not a dependent) and who is unable to pay for such reasonable and necessary expenses.

(III) In addition, for a debtor eligible for chapter 13, the debtor's monthly expenses may include the actual administrative expenses of administering a chapter 13 plan for the district in which the debtor resides, up to an amount of 10 percent of the projected plan payments, as determined under schedules issued by the Executive Office for the United States Trustees.

(IV) In addition, the debtor's monthly expenses may include the actual expenses for each dependent child less than 18 years of age, not to exceed $1,500 per year per child, to attend a private or public elementary or secondary school if the debtor provides documentation of such expenses and a detailed explanation of why such expenses are reasonable and necessary, and why such expenses are not already accounted for in the National Standards, Local Standards, or Other Necessary Expenses referred to in subclause (I).

(V) In addition, the debtor's monthly expenses may include an allowance for housing and utilities, in excess of the allowance specified by the Local Standards for housing and utilities issued by the Internal Revenue Service, based on the actual expenses for home energy costs if the debtor provides documentation of such actual expenses and demonstrates that such actual expenses are reasonable and necessary.

(iii) The debtor's average monthly payments on account of secured debts shall be calculated as the sum of—

(I) the total of all amounts scheduled as contractually due to secured creditors in each month of the 60 months following the date of the petition; and

(II) any additional payments to secured creditors necessary for the debtor, in filing a plan under chapter 13 of this title, to maintain possession of the debtor's primary residence, motor vehicle, or other property necessary for the support of the debtor and the debtor's dependents, that serves as collateral for secured debts;

(iv) The debtor's expenses for payment of all priority claims (including priority child support and alimony claims) shall be calculated as the total amount of debts entitled to priority, divided by 60.

[*11 U.S.C. §707(b)(2)(A) (ii), (iii), and (iv) (new text in italics)*]

Example B

Continuing with the facts in Example A, the debtor has estimated the following expenses:

National Standard for food, clothing, and other items, for household of four with monthly income $5,834 and over	$1,564
Additional amount for 5th household member	209
Transportation:	
First car	475
Second car	338
Operating costs	399
Housing and utilities	1,418
Health insurance	322
Support for debtor's disabled father	250
Chapter 13 fees	50
Special fees for one child with learning disabilities	350
Secured debt payments to be made monthly under the plan	500
Payment of priority tax claims	75
Total	$5,950

In Example A, the debtor's current monthly income (average of the previous 6 months) was $6,000; reduced by the average monthly deduction (monthly net income) of $5,950, results in a net income of $50 per month. As previously noted, since the net income is less than $100, the presumption is that no abuse exists. If the monthly net income had been equal to or greater than $100 and less than or equal to $166.66, abuse would have been presumed if the monthly net income times 60 was less than 25 percent of the debtor's nonpriority unsecured claims. Finally, if the monthly net income had been greater than $166.66, the presumption would have been that there was abuse. When an abuse exists, the debtor is not allowed to use chapter 7, and the petition will be dismissed unless the debtor agrees to convert the case to chapter 13 or chapter 11.

11.4 Rebutting the Presumption of Abuse

The presumption of abuse may only be rebutted by demonstrating special circumstances, such as a serious medical condition, or a call or order to active duty in the Armed Forces. To the extent such special circumstances justify additional expenses or adjustments of current monthly income for which there is no reasonable alternative, results in the debtor's circumstances not being construed to demonstrate abuse, the additional expenses will be allowed as provided in section 707(b)(2)(B):

> *(B) (i) In any proceeding brought under this subsection, the presumption of abuse may only be rebutted by demonstrating special circumstances, such as a serious medical condition or a call or order to active duty in the Armed Forces, to the extent such special circumstances that justify additional expenses or adjustments of current monthly income for which there is no reasonable alternative.*
>
> *(ii) In order to establish special circumstances, the debtor shall be required to itemize each additional expense or adjustment of income and to provide—*
>
> > *(I) documentation for such expense or adjustment to income; and*
> >
> > *(II) a detailed explanation of the special circumstances that make such expenses or adjustment to income necessary and reasonable.*
>
> *(iii) The debtor shall attest under oath to the accuracy of any information provided to demonstrate that additional expenses or adjustments to income are required.*

> *(iv) The presumption of abuse may only be rebutted if the additional expenses or adjustments to income referred to in clause (i) cause the product of the debtor's current monthly income reduced by the amount determined under clauses (ii), (iii), and (iv) of subparagraph (A) when multiplied by 60 to be less than the lesser of—*
>
> > *(I) 25 percent of the debtor's nonpriority unsecured claims, or $6,000, whichever is greater; or*
> >
> > *(II) $10,000.*

[*11 U.S.C. §707(b)(2)(B) (new text in italics)*]

Furthermore, Code section 707(b)(2)(D) provides that the provisions of the means test as previously described do not apply if the debtor is a disabled veteran and the indebtedness occurred primarily during a period when the debtor was on active duty:

> *(D) Subparagraphs (A) through (C) shall not apply, and the court may not dismiss or convert a case based on any form of means testing, if the debtor is a disabled veteran (as defined in section 3741(1) of title 38), and the indebtedness occurred primarily during a period during which he or she was—*
>
> > *(i) on active duty (as defined in section 101(d)(1) of title 10); or*
> >
> > *(ii) performing a homeland defense activity (as defined in section 901(1) of title 32).*

[*11 U.S.C. §707(b)(2)(D) (new text in italics)*]

11.5 Other Basis for Abuse or Dismissal

Code section 707(b)(6) provides that only the bankruptcy judge or U.S. trustee can also assert abuse if it is determined the petition was filed in bad faith or the totality of the circumstances of the debtor's financial situation demonstrates abuse as stipulated in Code section 707(b)(3):

> *(3) In considering under paragraph (1) whether the granting of relief would be an abuse of the provisions of this chapter in a case in which the presumption in subparagraph (A)(i) of such paragraph does not arise or is rebutted, the court shall consider—*

(A) whether the debtor filed the petition in bad faith; or

(B) the totality of the circumstances (including whether the debtor seeks to reject a personal services contract and the financial need for such rejection as sought by the debtor) of the debtor's financial situation demonstrates abuse.

[*11 U.S.C. §707(b)(3) (new text in italics)*]

Code section 707(c) provides that if it is in the best interest of a victim of a crime of violence or drug trafficking, the court may dismiss a voluntary case filed by the debtor convicted of such crime. However, the court may not dismiss the case if the debtor establishes by a preponderance of evidence that the filing under this chapter is necessary to satisfy a domestic support obligation.

Chapter 12

Impact on Consumer Bankruptcies

12.1 Introduction

Chapters 1 through 10 describe major changes to the Code by the Bankruptcy Abuse Prevention and Consumer Protection Act of 2005 (2005 Act) that affect businesses, and chapters 13 through 15 focus on the tax provisions in the 2005 Act. It is the consumer issues, however, that were driving the need for bankruptcy reform. This chapter briefly describes several of these key issues, and Chapter 11 focuses on the means testing—a process by which some debtors who have annual income above the state median income may be required to file chapter 11 or 13 because chapter 7 liquidation may no longer be available for their use.

12.2 Time Between Discharges (2005 Act Section 312)

Under an amendment to Code section 727(a)(8) affecting chapter 7 cases, the minimum time period between discharges is increased, from six years under previous Code provisions, to eight years under the 2005 Act. As a result, debtors will be denied discharge if a chapter 7 petition is filed within eight years of a prior discharge under either chapter 7 or chapter 11.

Changes to Code section 1328 indicate that under a chapter 13 petition, debtors will be denied discharge if discharge was granted in a prior case filed under chapter 7, 11, or 12 within 4 years of the chapter 13 order for relief, or, if discharge was granted in a prior case filed under chapter 13, within two years of the date of the current chapter 13 order.

12.3 Requirements for Tax Returns and Other Documents (2005 Act Section 315(b))

The 2005 Act modifies Code section 521 to add a number of new mandates regarding the submission (to the court, trustee, or other parties in interest as specified) of documents and other requirements from individual debtors under chapters 7, 11, and 13. Failure to submit such documents and related schedules on time within 45 days of filing will result in automatic dismissal (one 45-day extension allowed), unless the court orders otherwise. New requirements for documents (in addition to those existing prior to the 2005 Act) include:

- Certification of receipt and reading of informational notice by debtor
- Evidence of all payments received by debtor from employers within 60 days prior to petition filing
- Itemized statement of monthly net income
- Statement of reasonably anticipated increases in income or expenditures for 12 months after the date of filing

New requirements for filing tax returns and providing copies or transcripts include:

- Copies of the federal income tax return (or a transcript of the return) for the year most recently due for which a return was filed must be provided to the trustee and any creditor submitting a timely request, at least seven days before the Code section 341 meeting.
- On the request of a party in interest or the court, individual debtors must also file with the court a copy or transcript of the following returns at the same time filed with the IRS: tax returns for each year ending while the case is pending; tax returns for a tax year ending during the three years prior to filing; and any amendments filed to these returns.

12.4 Credit and Budget Briefing and Instruction (2005 Act Section 106)

According to Code section 109(h), individuals may not be a debtor in bankruptcy unless they have received a credit and budget briefing from an approved nonprofit agency during the 180-day period prior to the filing of the petition by the individual. Such courses must be approved by the U.S. trustee or bankruptcy administrator for each district under standards in the 2005 Act, and the clerk of the court must maintain a list of approved services for debtor reference. The required briefing may take place in a group or individual setting, including by telephone or on the Internet; must outline the opportunities available for credit counseling and assist the individual in performing budget analysis; and must be provided regardless of ability to pay for such services. Debtors must submit a certificate from the approved agency describing the services received and any debt repayment plan developed with the agency's assistance.

Credit briefing is not required in situations where the debtor resides in a district where there are no agencies approved as adequate by the U.S. trustee, or where, due to exigent circumstances, the debtor was forced to file for immediate relief and sought but was unable to obtain a briefing within at least five days prior to filing (in which cases the briefing must occur within 30 days after filing). Other circumstances exempting the debtor from the credit briefing are incapacity, disability, or active military duty in a military combat zone (*incapacity* means the debtor is incapable of realizing rational decisions with respect to his financial responsibilities by reason of mental illness or mental deficiency; *disability* means the debtor is so physically impaired as to be unable, after reasonable effort, to participate in an in-person, telephone, or Internet briefing).

Once they have entered bankruptcy, debtors in both chapter 7 and 13 must complete "an instructional course concerning personal financial management" to be eligible for discharge. The requirements and exceptions described in the above two paragraphs with respect to credit briefings generally also apply to the instructional course requirement. In conjunction with this requirement for education of the debtor, the 2005 Act includes provisions for the Executive Director of the Office for U.S. Trustees to develop and test a curriculum on financial management to help individual debtors manage their finances. These materials must be developed, tested, and evaluated and a report presented to Congress within 30 months or less of the enactment of 2005 Act section 106. (It would be interesting to see whether Congress itself might benefit from having to review such a curriculum on financial management.)

12.5 Limit on Automatic Stay (2005 Act Sections 302, 303, 311, and 315)

The 2005 Act made several changes to the Code that limit the impact of the automatic stay where there are bad faith or abusive filings. Code section 362(b)(22) and (23) were modified first to allow the continuance of any eviction proceeding to which the landlord had obtained prior to the filing of the petition a judgment of possession of such property and second to except the eviction proceeding from the stay if endangerment or illegal use of controlled substances under certain conditions.

12.6 Homestead Exemption (2005 Act Sections 308, 322, and 330)

Another area that has been quite controversial is the homestead exemption and associated issues. While Code section 522 allows the debtor to retain certain exempt assets, these assets go into the estate. Under Code section 522, a decision has to be made as to whether the property qualifies for one of the exemptions under Code section 522 or under applicable state law. Under Code section 522(b) the debtor may elect to use the federal exemptions provided in Code section 522(d) or the exemptions allowed by the state, unless the debtor's state of domicile requires the state law exemptions to be followed. A majority of states require debtors to use the state exemptions.

The 2005 Act modified Code section 522(b)(3)(A) to provide that, subject to subsections (o) and (p), the determination of which state to use for the purpose of exemption depends on the state in which the debtor resided two years before the petition was filed. If the debtor's domicile was located in the same state for 730 days prior to filing, the exemption laws of that state would apply. However, if the debtor's domicile was in more than one state during this time period, the exemption laws in the state where the debtor lived 180 days prior to the beginning of the 730 day period would apply. If the debtor lived in more than one state during the 180 day period, the debtor would use the state where the debtor lived for a longer portion of the 180 days. The reason for the addition of the two-year residency requirement is to preclude debtors from moving prior to filing to a state with more favorable exemption laws. For example, some states such as Florida, Texas and Kansas, do not have a dollar cap on homestead exemptions. To take advantage of the law in the state of Florida, under the 2005 Act the debtor would have to live in Florida for at least two years prior to filing.

Subsection (o) of Code section 522 reduces the value of a residence or homestead to the extent that such value is attributable to any portion of any property that the debtor disposed of in the 10 years prior to the filing of the petition with the intent to hinder, delay, or defraud a creditor that the debtor could not exempt.

Subsection (p) of Code section 522 limits any value in a residence or homestead that was acquired during the 1,215-day period prior to the filing of the petition to $125,000. This provision does not apply to a family farmer or to a transfer of another homestead in the same state. Subsection "q" applies the $125,000 cap if the debtor has been convicted of a felony that demonstrates that the filing of the case was an abuse of the provisions of the Code or if the debtor owes a debt arising from any violation of the federal securities laws, state securities laws, fraud or manipulation in a fiduciary capacity, racketeering, or criminal or reckless misconduct that caused serious physical injury or death of another individual in the preceding five years. This limitation does not apply to the extent the interest in the homestead exemption is reasonably necessary for the support of the debtor or dependents of the debtor.

The Bankruptcy Code has a very comprehensive definition of property of the estate of a debtor. Section 541(a) of the Bankruptcy Code includes in the estate all legal and equitable interests of the debtor, wherever located and by whomever held.

12.7 Retirement Plans (2005 Act Section 224)

Section 541(c)(1) states that property of the debtor will be included in the estate notwithstanding any provision in an agreement or applicable nonbankruptcy law that restricts or conditions such a transfer, including those that provide that property reverts to a creditor conditioned on the bankruptcy, financial condition, or insolvency of the debtor.

One exception to this treatment is in Code section 541(c)(2), which states, "[A] restriction on the transfer of a beneficial interest of the debtor in a trust that is enforceable under applicable nonbankruptcy law is enforceable in a case under this title." The legislative history of the Bankruptcy Code indicates this exception was intended to keep the assets of any spendthrift trust of which the debtor was a beneficiary out of the debtor's estate in recognition of the wishes of the settler. The Supreme Court held the phrase "applicable non-bankruptcy law" in section 541(c)(2) of the Bankruptcy Code should be read to encompass any other law that might restrict the transfer of property to the estate.[1]

The Supreme Court in *Rousey v. Jacoway*[2] looked at the extent to which individual retirement accounts could be exempt property. As exempt property, the value in the accounts would not be considered property of the estate. Code section 522(d)(10)(E) provides that a debtor may withdraw from the estate his or her "right to receive . . . a payment under a stock bonus, pension, profit sharing, annuity, or similar plan or contract on account of . . . age." Several years after the Rouseys rolled over distributions from their pension plans into IRAs, they filed a joint chapter 7 bankruptcy petition.

Because the Code does not define the listed plans, the Supreme Court noted that "the Court looks to their ordinary meaning." The question that the Supreme Court dealt with was, is the Rouseys' IRA plan similar to the description in Code section 522(d)(10)(E)? The Court concluded:

> [T]he income the Rouseys will derive from their IRAs is likewise income that substitutes for wages lost upon retirement is demonstrated by the facts that (1) regulations require distribution to begin no later than the calendar year after the year the accountholder turns; (2) taxation of IRA money is deferred until the year in which it is distributed; (3) withdrawals before age 59 are subject to the 10 percent penalty; and (4)

[1] *Patterson v. Shuate*, 504 U.S. 753 (1992).
[2] 125 S. Ct. 1561 (2005).

> failure to take the requisite minimum distributions results in a 50 percent tax penalty on funds improperly remaining in the account.

The Rouseys can exempt IRA assets from the bankruptcy estate because the IRAs fulfill both of the Code section 522(d)(10)(E) requirements at issue here: They confer a right to receive payment on account of age and they are similar plans or contracts to those enumerated in Code section 522(d)(10)(E).

The 2005 Act added subsection 522(a)(2)(C) to permit a debtor to exempt certain retirement funds to the extent that the funds are in an account that is exempt from taxation under IRC section 401, 403, 408, 408A, 414, 457 or 501(a). IRC section 408 and 408A deal with individual retirement accounts and Roth retirement accounts. The 2005 Act added new Code subsection 522(n), which caps the amount that can be exempted from the estate of the debtor at $1,000,000:

> *(n) For assets in individual retirement accounts described in section 408 or 408A of the Internal Revenue Code of 1986, other than a simplified employee pension under section 408(k) of such Code, the aggregate value of such assets exempted under this section, without regard to amounts attributable to rollover contributions under section 402(c), 402(e)(6), 403(a)(4), 403(a)(5), and 403(b)(8) of the Internal Revenue Code of 1986, and earnings thereon, shall not exceed $1,000,000 in a case filed by a debtor who is an individual, except that such amount may be increased if the interests of justice so require.*

[*11 U.S.C. §522(n) (new text in italics)*]

While the 2005 Act amendments clearly provide that individual retirement accounts can be exempted from the estate, the 2005 Act also places a cap on the amount that can be excluded.

12.8 Chapter 13 (2005 Act Sections 102(h), 213, 306(b), 309(c), 317, 318, and 327)

The 2005 Act significantly affected chapter 13 in several key areas. Changes affecting tax issues relevant to chapter 13 are discussed in other parts of this book (see 13.8 and 14.7). Several of the most important non-tax measures are described here.

(a) Duration of Chapter 13 Plan

Prior to the 2005 Act, payments under a chapter 13 plan were generally spread over a three-year period; with court approval for cause, the period could be extended to five years. The 2005 Act modified Code section 1322(d) to require debtors with an annual income equal to or greater than the applicable median family income to spread payments over a period of at least five years unless full payment of claims occurs earlier. The 2005 Act did not change the payment period for debtors with annual income less than the applicable median income.

(b) Confirmation of Chapter 13 Plans

The 2005 Act makes several modifications of Code section 1325 dealing with confirmation requirements.

Retention of Lien

If a holder of a secured claim has accepted the plan, the holder retains the lien until the debt has been paid or until the debt is discharged under Code section 1328. If the case is dismissed or converted without completion of the plan, the creditor retains the lien. Additionally, if the property to be distributed under the plan is in the form of periodic payments in equal monthly amounts, the amount of the payments must be large enough to provide adequate payment during the period of plan payments.

If the lien arising from a purchase money security interest was in an automobile that was acquired within 910 days prior to the petition, or if the collateral for that debt incurred during the one-year period prior to filing consists of any other thing of value, the section 506 provision requiring separation of the debt into secured and unsecured parts does not apply. Thus the creditor retains its lien until the debt is paid in full even if the value of the collateral is less than the amount of the claim at plan confirmation date.

Additional Confirmation Requirements

The 2005 Act added to the list in Code section 1325(a) the following three requirements:

> *(7) the action of the debtor in filing the petition was in good faith; and*
>
> *(8) the debtor has paid all amounts that are required to be paid under a domestic support obligation and that first become payable after the date of the filing of the petition if the debtor is required by a judicial or administrative order, or by statute, to pay such domestic support obligation.*
>
> *(9) the debtor has filed all applicable Federal, State, and local tax returns as required by section 1308.*

[*11 U.S.C. §1325(a) (new text in italics)*]

Disposable Income

Section 1325(b) provides that if the plan is objected to by the trustee or a holder of an unsecured claim, the court may not approve the plan unless the value of the property to be distributed is not less than the amount of the claim or all of the debtor's projected disposable income to be received in the applicable commitment period be applied to make payments to the unsecured creditors. The term *disposable income* as defined in Code section 1325(b)(2) "means current monthly income received by the debtor (other than child support payments, foster care payments, or disability payments for a dependent child made in accordance with applicable nonbankruptcy law to the extent reasonably necessary to be expended for such child) less amounts reasonably necessary to be expended" for the support of a dependent, based on Code section 707(b)(2) (and as described in chapter 13), for charitable contributions and for payments necessary for the continuation, preservation, and operation of a business for a debtor engaged in business.

12.9 Chapter 11 Cases Filed by Individuals (2005 Act Section 321)

As noted in chapter 11, if an individual debtor filing is determined to be abusive, the chapter 7 petition will be dismissed unless the debtor coverts it to chapter 11 or 13. To provide at least some similarities between chapters 11 and 13, the Code modified chapter 11 to make the proceedings for individuals similar to those in chapter 13. For tax purposes this change has created several problems because a separate bankruptcy estate is created when a chapter 11 petition is filed by an individual, but not when a chapter 13 petition is filed. It is expected that the IRS will issue some guideline to handle these tax problems. The major changes to chapter 11 are described here.

(a) Property Acquired Postpetition Including Earnings

Code section 1115 is modified by the following provision:

> *(a) In a case in which the debtor is an individual, property of the estate includes, in addition to the property specified in section 541—*
>
> > *(1) all property of the kind specified in section 541 that the debtor acquires after the commencement of the case but before the case is closed, dismissed, or converted to a case under chapter 7, 12, or 13, whichever occurs first; and*

> *(2) earnings from services performed by the debtor after the commencement of the case but before the case is closed, dismissed, or converted to a case under chapter 7, 12, or 13, whichever occurs first.*
>
> *(b) Except as provided in section 1104 or a confirmed plan or order confirming a plan, the debtor shall remain in possession of all property of the estate.*

[*11 U.S.C. §1115(a) and (b) (new text in italics)*]

Thus, all property and earnings of the individual debtor become property of the estate. In chapter 13, debtors continue to file their own tax returns and no separate estate is created; the opposite is true in chapter 11, where there is a separate estate. From a tax perspective, the problems created by this difference are significant. For personal services, the employee will continue to receive a W-2 form reporting earnings, yet the earnings are property of the estate. Until some form of explanation is received from the IRS, considerable uncertainty exists as to how to account for the income earned by individual debtors. One option is to report the income on the tax return filed by the estate, if in fact the earnings go to the estate as specified by the Code section 1155. Individual debtors would report on their tax return any funds that the estate disbursed to them for living and other related expenses. The disbursement of these funds by the estate should be based on an order issued by the bankruptcy court. Most likely these disbursements would be reported by the estate on Form 1099 and deducted by the estate as an administrative expense. Under this option, it would appear that the estate would be entitled to the tax benefit associated with the withholdings and the debtor would be responsible for any taxes that are due on the disbursements received from the estate. In this case the court would need to allow the tax payments as a necessary administrative expense in determining the amount to be used for living expenses.

Another option is to have individual debtors report these earnings on their individual income tax returns. Any payments to the estate would then be allowed as a deduction for adjusted gross income. Alternatively, a better option may be for the estate to not report the receipts as income because the estate is simply receiving property from the debtor that is not subject to a tax. Such payments could be considered payments of debt and thus would not be subject to a deduction.

To avoid some of these issues, the IRC might be modified to provide that a separate estate is not created for chapter 11, but additional problems would be created.

(b) Future Earnings in Plan

A new paragraph is added to Code section 1123(a) making it mandatory for an individual to provide future income earned by the individual as part of the funding of a plan. Code section 1123(a)(8) as modified provides:

> *(8) in a case in which the debtor is an individual, provide for the payment to creditors under the plan of all or such portion of earnings from personal services performed by the debtor after the commencement of the case or other future income of the debtor as is necessary for the execution of the plan.*

[*11 U.S.C. §1123(a) (new text in italics)*]

(c) Plan Confirmation

A new paragraph is added to Code section 1129(a) requiring the debtor to include in the plan at least a five-year minimum contribution of disposable income as defined in Code section 1325(b) (see 12.8 above) when an unsecured creditor objects.

> *(15) In a case in which the debtor is an individual and in which the holder of an allowed unsecured claim objects to the confirmation of the plan—*
>
> > *(A) the value, as of the effective date of the plan, of the property to be distributed under the plan on account of such claim is not less than the amount of such claim; or*
> >
> > *(B) the value of the property to be distributed under the plan is not less than the projected disposable income of the debtor (as defined in section 1325(b)(2)) to be received during the 5-year period beginning on the date that the first payment is due under the plan, or during the period for which the plan provides payments, whichever is longer.*

[*11 U.S.C. §1129(a)(15) (new text in italics)*]

(d) Domestic Support Obligations

In dealing with the cramdown of an unsecured creditor, Code section 1129(b)(2)(B)(ii) is modified to allow domestic support obligations to be paid outside of the general rules related to priority of claims under the fair and equitable provisions of the Code.

(e) Discharge of Debts

A new paragraph is added to Code section 1141(d) providing that an individual debtor will receive a discharge only after completion of the payments under the plan.

The 2005 Act modified Code section 1141(d)(5) to provide:

> *(5) In a case in which the debtor is an individual—*
>
> *(A) unless after notice and a hearing the court orders otherwise for cause, confirmation of the plan does not discharge any debt provided for in the plan until the court grants a discharge on completion of all payments under the plan;*
>
> *(B) at any time after the confirmation of the plan, and after notice and a hearing, the court may grant a discharge to the debtor who has not completed payments under the plan if—*
>
> *(i) the value, as of the effective date of the plan, of property actually distributed under the plan on account of each allowed unsecured claim is not less than the amount that would have been paid on such claim if the estate of the debtor had been liquidated under chapter 7 on such date; and*
>
> *(ii) modification of the plan under section 1127 is not practicable; and . . .*

[*11 U.S.C. §1141(d)(5) (new text in italics)*]

(f) Plan Modification

The 2005 Act added subsection (e) to Code section 1127 allowing individuals to modify their plan at any time prior to the completion of payments upon request by the debtor, trustee, U.S. trustee, or allowed unsecured creditor. The modification may involve the amount, time, and under certain conditions the distribution to creditors. Proper disclosure must be made of any modifications under the provisions of Code section 1125. Code section 1127(e) and (f) provides:

> *(e) If the debtor is an individual, the plan may be modified at any time after confirmation of the plan but before the completion of payments under the plan, whether or not the plan has been substantially consummated, upon request of the debtor, the trustee, the United States trustee, or the holder of an allowed unsecured claim, to—*

(1) increase or reduce the amount of payments on claims of a particular class provided for by the plan;

(2) extend or reduce the time period for such payments; or

(3) alter the amount of the distribution to a creditor whose claim is provided for by the plan to the extent necessary to take account of any payment of such claim made other than under the plan.

(f) (1) Sections 1121 through 1128 and the requirements of section 1129 apply to any modification under subsection (a).

(2) The plan, as modified, shall become the plan only after there has been disclosure under section 1125 as the court may direct, notice and a hearing, and such modification is approved.

[*11 U.S.C. §1127(e) and (f) (new text in italics)*]

12.10 Effective Date of Changes

Modification to the homestead exemptions applies to all cases filed on or after April 20, 2005. The other provisions generally apply to all petitions filed on or after October 17, 2005.

Chapter 13

Tax Determination and Discharge

13.1 Introduction

The Bankruptcy Abuse Prevention and Consumer Protection Act of 2005 (2005 Act) contains approximately 20 tax changes that required modifications of the Bankruptcy Code. Several of the provisions were recommendations made by the National Bankruptcy Review Commission based on a report prepared by the Tax Advisory Committee appointed by the Chairman of the National Bankruptcy Review Commission. However, a few of the provisions contradict the recommendations of both the National Bankruptcy Review Commission and the Tax Advisory Committee. In general most of the provisions selected from the recommendations of the report prepared by the National Review Commission and those added to the 2005 Act were favorable to the taxing authorities, especially to state and local taxing authorities. This chapter discusses those provisions relating to tax determination and discharge; Chapter 14 discusses the issues associated with filing tax returns, and Chapter 15 discusses the application of federal tax laws to state and local taxes. Changes to priority taxes were discussed in Chapter 5 (see section 5.3) and Chapter 9 (see sections 9.4 and 9.5) of this publication.

13.2 Treatment of Certain Liens (2005 Act Sections 701 and 711)

(a) Practice Prior to 2005 Act

Code section 724(b) now dictates that proceeds from property subject to an unavoidable tax lien shall be distributed to two other parties before the taxing authority gets any money. Under that scheme, all senior secured claims are paid and then the priority claimants identified in Code section 507(a)(1)-(7) are paid, but only to the extent of the amount of the tax claim secured by the lien. So, among others, in a chapter 7 following a failed chapter 11, the lawyers and accountants allowed administrative claims in the chapter 11 would be paid before the tax claims even though the taxing authority had perfected its tax lien.

(b) Changes Enacted

Tax liens arising from *ad valorem* tax on real or personal property of the estate will be specifically excepted from Code section 724(b)'s distribution pattern. Those tax liens will not be subordinated to any Code section 507 claims; however, all other tax liens will still be subordinated.

Even as to the remaining subordinated tax liens, amended Code section 724(b)(2) expressly excludes expenses incurred in a chapter 11 proceeding that are asserted as a priority claim in a subsequent chapter 7 from the scope of section 507(a)(1) for the purposes of distributions under Code section 724(b).

New Code section 724(e) imposes some marshalling requirements before a trustee can subordinate the tax liens, exhausting unencumbered property and recovering costs from secured creditors for preserving or disposing of their assets.

New Code section 724(f), while awkwardly worded, wants to say that *ad valorem* taxes can be subordinated to payment of wages claims under Code section 507(a)(4) and to claims for contributions to employee benefit plans under Code section 507(a)(5).

(c) Impact of Change

Local taxing authorities move with mechanical diligence and compelling regularity in perfecting liens to secure payment of *ad valorem* taxes on real and personal property. Liens for *ad valorem* taxes will be perfected; money that was available under prior law to satisfy priority claimants will no longer be available.

In the greater scheme of things, paying secured *ad valorem* tax claims makes a great deal of sense. However, another amendment, noted immediately below, eliminates the ability of a bankruptcy court to consider the actual value of the property used to compute the amount of the *ad valorem* tax. Viewed with the removal of that authority, the change in subordination compels any potential priority claimant to define precisely how their claim will be satisfied, and what *ad valorem* taxes exist.

13.3 Determination of *ad valorem* Tax Liability (2005 Act Section 701(b))

(a) Practice Prior to 2005 Act

Under current Code section 505(a), a debtor or other party can object to the amount of any *ad valorem* tax. Specifically, such objection could be filed and heard by a bankruptcy court, even if the time for disputing the amount or validity of those taxes had expired under local law.

(b) Changes Enacted

New Code section 505(a)(2)(C) excepts *ad valorem* taxes from the bankruptcy court's authority to redetermine the amount of a tax liability if (but only if) the applicable period for contesting or redetermining the amount of that tax under any law (other than bankruptcy law) has expired.

(c) Impact of Changes

On its face, the amendment appears totally benign and quite logical. If the time to dispute the tax claim under applicable non-bankruptcy law has expired, why on earth should the bankruptcy court be able to change the amount of the tax? Why? Because debtors often ignore or are unaware of the time limitations to dispute the tax claim.

The answer lies in experience and reality. Financially struggling businesses deal first with their banks and their major vendors, not their tax obligations. Quite often, a debtor's assets have diminished in value. Therefore, the estate has a tax claim, based on a prior and higher value, that in no way relates to the current value of that asset in bankruptcy and the time to challenge that value has expired under local law. The taxing authority gets a windfall, higher tax based on a false value. The creditors, who could do nothing to dispute the tax claim in a non-bankruptcy setting, cannot challenge the tax claim in bankruptcy. The estate then becomes saddled with an *ad valorem* tax that is totally out of proportion to the value of the property.

The impact of this section must be viewed together with the prior amendment noted to Code section 724. By eliminating any dispute of the tax claims and removing subordination of payment for *ad valorem* taxes. For the moment, Congress has assured that local *ad valorem* taxes will be given a super priority, in comparison to the previous statute, and none of the creditors or other interested parties can dispute the amount of the tax. Over time, creditors, particularly vendors, will devise ways to secure their claims ahead of the *ad valorem* taxes.

13.4 Notice of Request to Determine Taxes (2005 Act, Section 703)

(a) Practice Prior to 2005 Act

Previously, there had been no centralized address list of governmental tax authorities for mailing requests and notices in bankruptcy cases.

(b) Changes Enacted

The Act contains a provision that requires the clerk of the court to maintain a list of addresses of Federal, State and local governmental units responsible for collection of taxes where services of requests are to be filed. The new requirements also provide that where a governmental unit does not designate an address or provide an address to the clerk, requests may be served at the address for the filing of a tax return or protest with the appropriate taxing authority of such governmental unit.

(c) Impact of Changes

The effect of the requirement that the court clerk maintain a list of various tax authorities will be to assist debtors and others with the filing documents at the address designated by the tax authorities who provide such information. From the perspective of the tax authorities, it will help insure that requests are routed to the unit responsible for bankruptcy related matters. The Act does not address how this list is to be compiled nor does it address how extensive the list must be to accommodate debtors who have tax filing requirements in multiple jurisdictions spread throughout the country.

13.5 Rate of Interest on Tax Claims (2005 Act Section 704)

(a) Practice Prior to 2005 Act

Code section 1129(a)(9) provided that the total value of the payment over a period not to exceed six years from the assessment date was to equal the amount of the tax claim as of the effective date of the plan. There was no other provision that specified an interest rate; not only was a market rate to be use for tax purposes but also for other claims. In fact, there was no provision in the Code that suggested or implied that a creditor should receive more than the value of its claim until Code section 511 was added by the 2005 Act.

(b) Changes Enacted

Section 704 of the 2005 Act adds new Code section 511 providing that if interest is required on a tax claim, including tax claims qualifying as administrative expenses, or to enable a creditor to receive the present value of the allowed amount of a tax claim, the rate of interest shall be the rate determined under applicable nonbankruptcy law. Code section 511 provides the following:

§511. Rate of interest on tax claims

(a) If any provision of this title requires the payment of interest on a tax claim or on an administrative expense tax, or the payment of interest to enable a creditor to receive the present value of the allowed amount of a tax claim, the rate of interest shall be the rate determined under applicable nonbankruptcy law.

(b) In the case of taxes paid under a confirmed plan under this title, the rate of interest shall be determined as of the calendar month in which the plan is confirmed.

[*11 U.S.C. §511 (new text in italics)*]

While Code section 511 indicates that the taxing authority should receive a payment of interest to enable a creditor to receive the present value of the allowed amount of a tax claim, the concept of value is distorted by the requirement that the nonbankruptcy rate must be used to determine value.

(c) Impact of Changes

As noted above, the Code does not specify the interest rate that is to be used for tax claims that are entitled to interest, but it does indicate that a market rate should be used. Judicial consensus is that the Federal statutory rate is relevant in determining the appropriate market rate of interest. To avoid wasting both judicial and debtor resources by litigating the rate, the National Bankruptcy Review Commission followed the recommendation of the Tax Advisory Committee that the rate be fixed at the statutory rate under IRC section 6621(a)(2), without reference to IRC section 6621(c) and that it should be the rate in effect as of the confirmation date. The rate under IRC section 6621 was included in early proposed modifications to the IRC, but was subsequently modified to include the federally applicable rate in section 1274(d). IRC section 1274 appeared to be a reasonable substitute. Subsequent drafts provided that IRC section 1274 would apply to federal taxes and other taxing units would use the rate under nonbankruptcy law. As passed, 2005 Act section 704 eliminates any reference to the Internal Revenue Code by providing that nonbankruptcy law applies to all taxes where interest is required.

While the rate for federal taxes approximates market value, the rate for state and local taxes could be in excess of 20 percent, resulting in state and local taxing authorities receiving interest in excess of market rate at the expense of other creditors. Additionally, it violates the general philosophy underlying bankruptcy law that creditors should not receive consideration in excess of the value of such claims.

13.6 The Stay of Tax Court Proceedings (2005 Act Section 709)

(a) Practice Prior to 2005 Act

In *Halpren v. Comm'r*, 96 T.C. 895 (1991), the United States Tax Court refused to hear a case involving taxable years ending after the voluntary petition was filed, citing section 362(a)(8), the subparagraph of the automatic stay prohibiting the commencement or continuation of a proceeding before the Tax Court. Read literally, that part of the automatic stay did in fact prohibit the initiation or continuation of any proceeding before the Tax Court after a bankruptcy was filed.

(b) Changes Enacted

Language was added to Code section 362(a)(8) to limit the stay, as to individuals, to proceedings for taxable periods "ending" before the entry of an order for relief in bankruptcy. For corporate debtors, the stay was limited to those taxable periods that a bankruptcy court might determine.

(c) Impact of Changes

This change is technical. The statute was "tweaked" to deal with a matter that needed to be resolved. As for corporate debtors, occasions may still arise where filing a Tax Court petition and also filing a complaint to determine a tax liability in the bankruptcy proceeding will be the more prudent course of action.

13.7 Discharge of the Estate's Liability for Unpaid Taxes (2005 Act Section 715)

(a) Practice Prior to 2005 Act

Code section 505(b) previously provided that a trustee may request a determination of any unpaid liability of the estate for any tax uncured during the administration of the case, by submitting a tax return for such tax and a request for a prompt determination to the governmental unit charged with collection or determination of tax liability. Unless the return was fraudulent or contains a material misrepresentation, the trustee, the debtor and any successor to the debtor are discharged from any liability for the tax reported on the return if paid and if the governmental unit did not notify the trustee, within 60 days, that such return has been selected for examination or, if selected for examination, the governmental unit does not complete the examination within 180 days or such additional time as the court permits.

(b) Changes Enacted

In addition, the Act adds "the estate" to the list of entities that can apply for a prompt determination of any unpaid tax liability of the estate.

(c) Impact of Changes

The addition of "the estate" to the list of entities that can apply for a prompt determination makes it clear that the estate, being the tax entity that requested the determination, is also covered by the determination. Thus an estate with funds will no longer be liable for any tax that may be subsequently assessed. In cases where there are multiple entities, this change will allow the trustee or debtor-in-possession to close or leave estates open when a letter is received indicating that the return has been accepted without concern of future action by the taxing authority.

13.8 No Discharge of Fraudulent Taxes in Chapter 13 (2005 Act Section 707)

Two major tax changes will affect the extent to which chapter 13 is used—one requires four years of tax returns and the other disallows certain taxes from being discharged that were previously discharged in chapter 13. See Chapter 14 of this publication, dealing with the requirement for tax returns to be filed in chapter 13.

The 2005 Act introduces substantial changes to the chapter 13 "super-discharge" found in Code section 1328(a). Under amended section 1398(a), the chapter 13 discharge now conforms to the chapter 7 discharge for individual debtors for purposes of so-called fraud taxes, that is, those taxes that are associated with a fraudulent return, non-filed or certain late-filed returns, and any attempt to willfully evade or defeat a tax in any manner. Thus, tax claims under Code section 523(a)(1) are now excepted from the chapter 13 discharge. In addition to the "fraud" tax claims, the 2005 Act includes the priority taxes found in Code section 507(a)(8) as those that would survive the chapter 13 discharge.

(a) Impact of Changes

While this change does eliminate the difference between the dischargeability of taxes under chapter 7 and chapter 13, it also eliminates the key reason why some debtors elected to file chapter 13. Chapter 13 as it existed prior to the 2005 Act facilitates the workout of tax claims and was consistent with other provisions of the 2005 Act that require taxpayers to pay some of their claims over the plan period. In fact, taxing authorities may have to collect substantial taxes because chapter 13 required that all priority taxes be paid during the plan period and it places on the tax rolls individuals that have not paid taxes in several years. Because of this change it is expected that fewer taxpayers will now voluntarily elect chapter 13.

On the other hand, for those taxpayers that qualify to remain in chapter 7 under the 2005 Act, prior year tax returns are often not filed and limited portions, if any, of the taxes are paid during the collection period. In the final analysis, taxing authorities may receive a very small percent of the taxes due and probably less than would have been received in chapter 13.

13.9 No Discharge of Fraudulent Taxes in Chapter 11 (2005 Act Section 708)

(a) Practice Prior to 2005 Act

A corporation was entitled to a fresh start and obtained a discharge under Code section 1141 of all debts not provided for in the plan. Priority claims including tax priority claims were required to be provided for in the plan under Code section 1129(a)(9).

(b) Changes Enacted

Code section 1141 defines the effect of confirmation of a chapter 11 plan and specifically discharges certain debts that arose before confirmation. The 2005 amendment excepts tax liabilities from a chapter 11 discharge if the debtor corporation made a fraudulent return or willfully attempted in any manner to evade or defeat that tax or duty. The new provision also excepts from discharge any debt incurred under false pretenses or by making a false statement in writing. The potential mischief this provision may cause cannot be overstated. This is the first provision that excepts from the chapter 11 discharge a corporate misconduct debt or any other debt that is generally not provided for in the plan.

(c) Impact of Changes

The problematic aspect of this new concept is that a corporation is a legal fiction; a corporation may act only through its officers and directors. Often, these "bad guys" are gone by the time the issue of nondischargeability arises. Thus, the drain on cash imposed by nondischargeable debts is shouldered by innocents, that is, the creditors and new equity in the reorganized debtor. Code section 362(b)(9) does not operate as a stay against "the making of an assessment for any tax and issuance of a notice and demand for payment of such an assessment (but any tax lien that would otherwise attach to property of the estate by reason of such an assessment shall not take effect unless such tax is a debt of the debtor that will not be discharged in the case and such property or its proceeds are transferred out of the estate to, or otherwise revested in, the debtor)." Because of this provision it appears that the taxing authority will be able to obtain a lien on emergence from chapter 11 in unsecured assets that otherwise would have been available to fund operations and provide payments to unsecured creditors.

13.10 Effective Date of Changes

As with most of the changes made by the 2005 Act, these changes are effective with respect to cases commenced on or after October 17, 2005.

Chapter 14

Tax Return Issues

14.1 Introduction

Several unresolved issues related to the filing of tax returns were addressed in the tax provisions in the Bankruptcy Abuse Prevention and Consumer Protection Act of 2005 (2005 Act), including the determination of the status of returns filed by tax authorities, the dismissal of petition for failure to file returns, the setoff of tax refunds, and the requirement that four years of returns must be filed by chapter 13 debtors.

14.2 Income Tax Returns Prepared by Tax Authorities (2005 Act Section 714)

(a) Practice Prior to 2005 Act

Code section 523 provided an exception to discharge of certain debts under Code sections 727, 1141, 1228(a), 1228(b) or 1328(b) of an individual debtor from an unsecured claim of a governmental unit for a tax measured by income or gross receipts where the debtor failed to file a return. Where the debtor "cooperated" in the preparation of a return by taxing authorities and signed the return, the signed documents have generally been accepted as meeting the filing requirement and discharge granted in such cases. Where the debtor has failed to cooperate in the preparation of a return by taxing authorities, the courts have refused to grant a discharge for such taxes.

(b) Changes Enacted

The exception to discharge provided by Code section 523 where a debtor has failed to file a return is amended to provide that tax returns prepared by taxing authorities under IRC section 6020(a) on behalf of a taxpayer who has assisted in the preparation of such return by providing enough information to complete it will qualify as a return for discharge purposes. The rule will *not* apply to returns where the taxpayer did not assist or generally did not cooperate with the IRS or other applicable taxing authority in the preparation of the return. Such returns are generally based on information obtained by taxing authorities from third parties under IRC section 6020(b).

The new rules provide that, "For purposes of this subsection, the term "return" means a return that satisfies the requirements of applicable nonbankruptcy law (including applicable filing requirements). Such term includes a return prepared pursuant to section 6020(a) of the Internal Revenue Code of 1986, or similar State or local law, or a written stipulation to a judgment or final order entered by a nonbankruptcy tribunal, but does not include a return made pursuant to section 6020(b) of the Internal Revenue Code of 1986, or similar State or local law."

(c) Impact of Changes

The practical effect of these changes is to codify what has been one of the criteria used by courts in a discharge determination involving what is generally referred to as a substitute for return prepared by taxing authorities. This change is consistent with how the IRS views returns prepared with the cooperation of the taxpayer as opposed to those where there has been lack of cooperation from the taxpayer.

14.3 Dismissal for Failure to Timely File Tax Returns (2005 Act Section 720)

The debtor must now timely file *postpetition* tax returns or suffer conversion or dismissal of the case. The conversion or dismissal is mandatory if the debtor does not file the returns or obtain an extension within 90 days after the taxing authority files its request. This provision applies in chapters 7, 11, 12, and 13. Although this provision is not jurisdictional—thus it may be waived in the appropriate circumstance—there is no doubt that this provision, along with others, is designed to limit the discretion of bankruptcy judges.

14.4 Payment of Taxes in the Conduct of Business (2005 Act Section 712)

(a) Practice Prior to 2005 Act

Prior to the 2005 Act, an application for allowance and payment of an administrative expense was required to be filed before being allowed administrative tax treatment.

(b) Changes Enacted

Any governmental entity can now be allowed administrative expense treatment for taxes incurred in the conduct of business after a petition in bankruptcy is filed without being required to file an application for allowance and for payment. Section 960, Title 28, makes officials, including the bankruptcy trustee, operating a business under the authority of a U.S. Court subject to all federal, state and local taxes applicable to such a business.

To clarify a trustee's duties regarding taxes, the amendments added two new paragraphs to section 960 that:

1. Require timely payment under nonbankruptcy law unless secured by a lien and abandoned within a reasonable period of time, or otherwise excused under a specific provision of Title 11.
2. Permit deferral of payment until a final distribution if a trustee under chapter 7 did not incur the tax or if the court makes determination of "probable insufficiency of funds" to pay in full all administrative expenses having an equal priority with the tax liability.

This amendment makes two additional changes in aid of state and local taxing authorities. The first change allows any expense authorized by "state statute," under which the claim arose, to be paid when the amount realized exceeds the amount of the secured claim. For example, if the state statute allowed attorney's fees or penalties for failure to pay, the amendment would permit payment of those amounts to the extent not considered a part of the secured claim.

The second change allows the trustee to recover property taxes from the sale proceeds as a necessary part of maintaining the property.

(c) Impact of Changes

As is true with several other tax changes included in the 2005 Act, the change will make it easier for state and local tax authorities to collect taxes. The impact on other creditors is minimized by the provision that, in a case pending under chapter 7, payments may be deferred until final distribution is made under Code section 726 of the Code, if the tax was incurred before the trustee was appointed, or before the due date of the return for which the court determines there is a probability the debtor will not be able to pay in full the administrative expenses and other claims with the same priority as the tax claim.

14.5 Tardily Filed Priority Tax Claims (2005 Act Section 713)

(a) Practice Prior to 2005 Act

Prior to the 2005 amendment, Code section 726 stated that a tardily filed claim, for the purposes of distribution, had to be filed before the date on which the trustee "commenced distribution" under Code section 726.

(b) Changes Enacted

The 2005 amendment adds a second part to the condition for the timely filing of a priority tax claim, namely that the taxing authority must file its claim before the *earlier* of 10 days after the mailing to creditors of the trustee's final report, *or* (the previously existing condition) the date on which the trustee commences *final* distribution. The word *final* was also added by the amendment; without this change, "any" distribution operated as the bar date for the filing of a priority tax claim.

(c) Impact of Changes

It is important that the claim be filed before the final order approving the trustee's report is entered to avoid requiring the trustee to recalculate the amount paid to creditors and equity holders, to rewrite the report, and to reschedule the hearings to approve the report. Filing a claim after the report is filed clearly affects the efficient court administration of the case. See *Pioneer Investment Servs. Co. v. New Brunswick Assocs., Ltd.*, 113 S. Ct. 1489 (1993). The provision as modified should satisfy the questions raised by trustees and provide for a more effective distribution.

14.6 Setoff of Tax Refund (2005 Act Section 718)

The 2005 Act excepts from the automatic stay the setoff of a refund and a liability, both of which have their origin in a prepetition taxable period unless the liability is disputed. If either the refund or the liability falls in the postpetition period, the setoff is stayed. If a setoff is tolled during a hearing to determine amount or legality of the tax, the taxing authority may freeze the refund.

(a) Impact of Change

This amendment reflects a procedure under local rule in existence in a large number of jurisdictions and should have minimal impact. However, it has been pointed out by some writers that the decision in *Seminole Tribe of Florida*, [116 S. Ct. 1114 (1996)] may preclude the debtor from recovering tax refunds that were setoff improperly by a state taxing authority.

14.7 Requirement to File Tax Returns to Confirm Chapter 13 Plans (2005 Act Section 716)

(a) Practice Prior to 2005 Act

There was no provision in the existing law that required a debtor to file federal, state or local tax returns in order to file under chapter 13 of the Code.

(b) Changes Enacted

To confirm a plan under chapter 13 of the Bankruptcy Code, a debtor must now file all applicable federal, state, and local tax returns as required by Code section 1308, which follows:

> ***§1308. Filing of prepetition tax returns***
>
> *(a) Not later than the day before the date on which the meeting of the creditors is first scheduled to be held under section 341(a), if the debtor was required to file a tax return under applicable nonbankruptcy law, the debtor shall file with appropriate tax authorities all tax returns for all taxable periods ending during the 4-year period ending on the date of the filing of the petition.*
>
> *(b) (1) Subject to paragraph (2), if the tax returns required by subsection (a) have not been filed by the date on which the meeting of creditors is first scheduled to be held under section 341(a), the trustee may hold open that meeting for a reasonable period of time to allow the debtor an additional period of time to file any unfiled returns, but such additional period of time shall not extend beyond—*
>
> *(A) for any return that is past due as of the date of the filing of the petition, the date that is 120 days after the date of that meeting; or*
>
> *(B) for any return that is not past due as of the date of the filing of the petition, the later of—*
>
> *(i) the date that is 120 days after the date of that meeting; or*
>
> *(ii) the date on which the return is due under the last automatic extension of time for filing that return to which the debtor is entitled, and for which request is timely made, in accordance with applicable nonbankruptcy law.*

(2) After notice and a hearing, and order entered before the tolling of any applicable filing period determined under this subsection, if the debtor demonstrates by preponderance of the evidence that the failure to file a return as required under this subsection is attributable to circumstances beyond the control of the debtor, the court may extend the filing period established by the trustee under this subsection for—

(A) a period of not more than 30 days for returns described in paragraph (1); and

(B) a period not to extend after the applicable extended due date for a return described in paragraph (2).

(c) For purposes of this section, the term "return" includes a return prepared pursuant to subsection (a) or (b) of section 6020 of the Internal Revenue Code of 1986, or a similar State or local law, or a written stipulation to a judgment or a final order entered by a nonbankruptcy tribunal.

[*11 U.S.C. §1308 (new text in italics)*]

Code section 1308 is a new section titled "Filing of Prepetition Tax Returns." This new section sets forth some time limits under which a debtor, where required under applicable nonbankruptcy law, must file with appropriate tax authorities all tax returns for all taxable periods ending during the four-year period ending on the date of the filing of the petition. The returns required under this section must be filed by the date of the first meeting of creditors or not more than 120 days afterward if such meeting is extended by the trustee if such returns are past due as of the date of the petition, or no later than the extended due date for any return if an extension of time for filing the return was timely made.

After a notice and hearing, and order entered before the tolling of any applicable filing period, if the debtor demonstrates that the failure to file a return as required is attributable to circumstances beyond the control of the debtor, the court may extend the filing period established by the trustee for not more than 30 days, not to exceed the extended due date for the return.

For purposes of this section, the term "returns" means a return prepared pursuant to section 6020(a) or (b) of the Internal Revenue Code of 1986, or a similar State or local law or a written stipulation to a judgment or final order entered by a nonbankruptcy tribunal.

Failure to file a tax return required under section 1308 will result in the dismissal or conversion of a case filed under chapter 13 to a case under chapter 7, whichever is in the best interest of the creditors and the estate.

(c) Impact of Changes

The effect of these changes will be to stimulate the filing of tax returns that may otherwise not be filed and to make it easier for tax agencies to collect taxes from debtors. The changes will also force taxpayers seeking protection under the Bankruptcy Code to comply with federal, state and local tax return filing requirements. For those debtors who for whatever reason do not have the information readily available or the funds for preparation of the tax returns, it will make it difficult or impossible for them to file bankruptcy. For example, a debtor who is unable to file a tax return for whatever reason and has income that is greater than the appropriate mean will have any chapter 7 petition that might be filed dismissed and will not be able to confirm a chapter 13 plan, resulting in the dismissal of a chapter 13 petition as well.

14.8 Effective Date of Changes

As with most of the changes made by the 2005 Act, these changes are effective with respect to cases commenced on or after October 17, 2005.

Chapter 15

State and Local Taxes

15.1 Introduction

Code section 346 is to generally follow the same provisions that apply for federal income tax purposes. Considerable conflicts existed between state and local taxes and federal taxes. Congress indicated at the time the Bankruptcy Reform Act of 1978 became law that the state and local tax issues would be changed when the Congress passed the federal bankruptcy tax laws. A few years later, Congress passed the Bankruptcy Tax Act of 1980 but no action was taken until 2005 (the Bankruptcy Abuse Prevention and Consumer Protection Act of 2005) to eliminate the tax problems that arose because of differences between the two federal laws. To correct these problems, the amendment to Code section 346 was written to conform Code section 346 to the provisions of the IRC including sections 1398, 1399, 108, and 1017.

15.2 Bankruptcy Estates (2005 Act Section 719)

(a) Practice Prior to 2005 Act

Code sections 346, 728, 1146 and 1231 outline special state and local tax provisions applying to individual and business cases. In many instances the tax treatment under these provisions does not coincide with federal tax provisions of the IRC.

Individual Cases—Chapters 7, 11, or 12

IRC section 1398 governs the income taxation of individual chapter 7 and 11 bankruptcy cases. Pursuant to this section a new taxpaying entity, the bankruptcy estate, comes into existence upon the filing of a petition for an individual under chapter 7 or 11 of the U. S. Bankruptcy Code. The bankruptcy estate succeeds to and takes into account specific tax attributes of the debtor, determined as of the first day of the debtor's taxable year in which the case commences, including net operating loss carryovers, charitable contributions carryovers, recovery of tax benefit items, credit carryovers, capital loss carryovers, basis, holding period and character of assets, method of accounting, suspended passive activity losses and credits, and suspended "at-risk" losses. Subject to minimum income thresholds, the bankruptcy estate is required to file income tax returns and pay income taxes on its taxable income. Taxable income of the estate is computed in the same manner as for an individual. Tax liability is determined under the regular income tax provisions that apply to married individuals filing separately. The income tax liability incurred by the estate becomes an administrative claim in the bankruptcy case.

For state and local income tax purposes, for cases involving individuals who file chapters 7, 11 or 12 bankruptcies, income of the estate is taxable to the estate—not to the debtor. The estate is required to use the same accounting method the debtor used immediately before the commencement of the case. If such individual is a partner in a partnership, any postpetition income from the partnership is generally taxable to the estate. In contrast to the federal provisions, which tax the estate as a married individual filing separately, the estate is taxed as an estate for state and local purposes.

The trustee assigned to a chapter 7 or 11 case or a debtor-in-possession in a chapter 11 case is required to withhold and make appropriate payments of state and local taxes on payment of claims for wages, salaries, commission, dividends, interest, or other payments.

No gain or loss is recognized on the transfer of property from the debtor to the estate. The estate succeeds to the character, basis, and holding period in assets transferred from the debtor. Property transferred from the estate to the debtor, other than through a sale, results in no gain or loss to the estate.

The tax attributes to which the estate succeeds are all-inclusive for state and local purposes, while for federal purposes, the tax attributes to which the estate is entitled are limited to a specific list of items (see IRC section 1398(g)). The estate may carry back losses to prepetition tax years of the debtor, whereas the debtor is only allowed to carry back losses to any postpetition tax year that arise after the case is closed. Any tax attribute transferred to the estate that remains unused will transfer back to the debtor subject to reduction from any cancellation of indebtedness that occurs pursuant to the bankruptcy upon the conclusion of the case.

Under general income tax law, income is realized upon the satisfaction of indebtedness for an amount that is less than the full amount of the obligation. However for federal purposes, pursuant to safe harbors provided in IRC section 108, gross income does not include any amount that would be includible in gross income by reason of the discharge of indebtedness of the taxpayer if the discharge occurs in a Title 11 (bankruptcy) case. Rather, net operating losses, general business credits, minimum tax credits, capital loss carryovers, adjusted tax basis of assets, passive activity losses and credits carryovers, and foreign tax credit carryovers are reduced. The operating rules for this required attribute reduction are found in IRC sections 108 and 1017 and the regulations thereunder.

For state and local income tax purposes, when a discharge of indebtedness occurs in a bankruptcy case, such income is not recognized by the estate, the debtor or a successor to the debtor. Net operating losses, including net operating loss carryovers, are reduced by the amount of the excludable discharge of indebtedness income. No income from discharge of indebtedness is realized where the indebtedness that was discharged consisted of items of a deductible nature that were not deducted or resulted in an expired net operating loss carryover or other deduction that did not offset income for any taxable period or contribute to a net operating loss. To the extent the amount of excludable discharge of indebtedness income exceeds the amount of net operating loss reduction required above, the basis of the debtor's property shall be reduced by the amount of the remaining excludable discharge of indebtedness income. The reduction in the aggregate basis of property is limited to the aggregate total liabilities remaining after the discharge of indebtedness.

For federal purposes, an individual debtor who files a chapter 7 or 11 case can make an irrevocable election to terminate his or her tax year as of the day preceding the day he or she files bankruptcy. When the election is made, the debtor will be required to file a tax return for two short return periods, the first of which will begin on January 1 for a calendar year taxpayer and end on the day preceeding the date the case commenced. The second short year will begin on the date the bankruptcy case commenced and end on December 31. The election must be timely filed with the IRS in order for the tax year of the debtor to be divided into prepetition and postpetition periods [See IRC §1398(d)]. For state and local purposes, the debtor's tax year is automatically split into two short year periods pursuant to provisions of the Bankruptcy Code. The ending date for the first short period is the date the bankruptcy case commences which differs by one day from the applicable date for federal purposes.

Unlike federal filing requirements which are based on a gross income filing threshold, state and local income tax returns for individual chapter 7 estates are required to be filed only if the estate has net taxable income for the entire period of administration of the chapter 7 case.

Individual Cases—Chapter 12 and Chapter 13 Cases

In chapter 13 cases, income of both the estate and the debtor are taxable to the debtor—not to the estate. No new entity is created when an individual files a chapter 12 or chapter 13 case.

Corporations and Partnerships

Pursuant to IRC section 1399, for federal income tax purposes, no separate taxable entity shall result from the filing of a bankruptcy petition on behalf of a corporation or partnership including an LLC or LLP.

State and local income tax laws generally apply to corporations and partnerships, including LLCs or LLPs in bankruptcy as though no case had been commenced. In chapter 7 corporate cases, state and local income tax returns for corporations in chapter 7 were required to be filed only if the corporation had net taxable income for the entire chapter 7 administrative period of the case.

(b) Changes Enacted

§346. Special provisions *related to the treatment of State and local taxes*

(a) Whenever the Internal Revenue Code of 1986 provides that a separate taxable estate or entity is created in a case concerning a debtor under this title, and the income, gain, loss, deductions, and credits of such estate shall be taxed to or claimed by the estate, a separate taxable estate is also created for purposes of any State and local law imposing a tax on or measured by income and such income, gain, loss, deductions, and credits shall be taxed to or claimed by the estate and may not be taxed to or claimed by the debtor. The preceding sentence shall not apply if the case is dismissed. The trustee shall make tax returns of income required under any such State or local law.

(b) Whenever the Internal Revenue Code of 1986 provides that no separate taxable estate shall be created in a case concerning a debtor under this title, and the income, gain, loss, deductions, and credits of an estate shall be taxed to or claimed by the debtor, such income, gain, loss, deductions, and credits shall be taxed to or claimed by the debtor under a State or local law imposing a tax on or measured by income *and may not be taxed to or claimed by the estate. The trustee shall make such tax returns of income of corporations and of partnerships as are required under any State or local law, but with respect to partnerships, shall make such returns only to the extent such returns are also required to be made under such Code. The estate shall be liable for any tax imposed on such corporation or partnership, but not for any tax imposed on partners or members.*

(c) With respect to a partnership or any entity treated as a partnership under a State or local law imposing a tax on or measured by income that is a debtor in a case under this title, any gain or loss resulting from a distribution of property from such partnership, or any distributive share of any income, gain, loss, deduction, or credit of *a partner or member* that is distributed, or considered distributed, from such partnership, after the commencement of the case, is gain, loss, income, deduction, or credit, as the case may be, of the *partner or member, and if such partner or member is a debtor in a case under this title, shall be subject to tax in accordance with subsection (a) or (b).*

(d) For purposes of any State or local law imposing a tax on or measured by income, the taxable period of a debtor in a case under this title shall terminate only if and to the extent that the taxable period of such debtor terminates under the Internal Revenue Code of 1986.

(e) The estate in *any* case *described in subsection (a)* shall use the same accounting method as the debtor used immediately before the commencement of the case, *if such method of accounting complies with applicable non-bankruptcy tax law.*

(f) For purposes of any State or local law imposing a tax on or measured by income, *a transfer of property from the debtor to the estate or from the estate to the debtor shall not be treated as a disposition for purposes of any provision assigning tax consequences to a disposition, except to the extent that such transfer is treated as a disposition under the Internal Revenue Code of 1986.*

(g) Whenever a tax is imposed pursuant to a State or local law imposing a tax on or measured by income pursuant to subsection (a) or (b), such tax shall be imposed at rates generally applicable to the same types of entities under such State or local law.

(h) The trustee shall withhold from any payment of claims for wages, salaries, commissions, dividends, interest, or other payments, or collect, any amount required to be withheld or collected under applicable State or local tax law, and shall pay such withheld or collected amount to the appropriate governmental unit at the time and in the manner required by such

tax law, and with the same priority as the claim from which such amount was withheld or *collected* was paid.

(*i*) *(1) To the extent that any State or local law imposing a tax on or measured by income provides for the carryover of any tax attribute from one taxable period to a subsequent taxable period, the estate shall succeed to such tax attribute in any case in which such estate is subject to tax under subsection (a).*

(2) After such a case is closed or dismissed, the debtor shall succeed to any tax attribute to which the estate succeeded under paragraph (1) *to the extent consistent with the Internal Revenue Code of 1986.*

(3) *The* estate may carry back any loss *or tax attribute* to a taxable period of the debtor that ended before *the date of* the order for relief under *this title to the extent that—*

(A) applicable State or local tax law provides for a carryback in the case of the debtor; and (B) the same or a similar tax attribute may be carried back by the estate to such a taxable period of the debtor under the Internal Revenue Code of 1986.

(j) (1) *For purposes of any State or local law imposing a tax on or measured by income,* income is not realized by the estate, the debtor, or a successor to the debtor by reason of discharge of indebtedness, *if any, that such income is subject to tax under the Internal Revenue Code of 1986.*

(2) Whenever the Internal Revenue Code of 1986 provides that the amount excluded from gross income in respect of the discharge of indebtedness in a case under this title shall be applied to reduce the tax attributes of the debtor or the estate, a similar reduction shall be made under any State or local law imposing a tax on or measured by income to the extent such State or local law recognizes such attributes. Such State or local law may also provide for the reduction of other attributes to the extent that the full amount of income from the discharge of indebtedness has not been applied.

> *(k) (1) Except as provided in this section and section 505, the time and manner of filing tax returns and the items of income, gain, loss, deduction, and credit of any taxpayer shall be determined under applicable nonbankruptcy law.*
>
> *(2) For Federal tax purposes, the provisions of this section are subject to the Internal Revenue Code of 1986 and other applicable Federal nonbankruptcy law.*

[*11 U.S.C. §346 (new text in italics)*]

Code section 1146(a) and (b) dealing with the short tax year and subsequent year returns was repealed because these provisions are not provided for in revised Code section 347. Likewise, Code section 728 is also repealed for the same reason.

Code section 1146(c), providing that a transfer of securities under Code section 1129 may not be taxed by any law imposing a stamp tax or similar tax, was not repealed but continues in effect as Code section 1146(a). Code section 1146(d), authorizing the proponent of a plan to request a determination for state and local tax purposes, limited to questions of law, of the tax effects of a plan also was not repealed, but continues in effect as Code section 1146(b). Code section 1231 was also modified in a similar manner to Code section 1146 except that the determination of the tax effect of the plan applies to any governmental unit and not just a state or local taxing authority. This change was not made to Code section 1146(b). However, the extent to which the federal tax may be determined may be limited by the reference to Code section 346. The revised Code section 1231 is as follows:

> *(b) The court may authorize the proponent of a plan to request a determination, limited to questions of law, by any governmental unit charged with responsibility for collection or determination of a tax on or measured by income, of the tax effects, under section 346 of this title and under the law imposing such tax, of the plan. In the event of an actual controversy, the court may declare such effects after the earlier of—*
>
> *(1) the date on which such governmental unit responds to the request under this subsection; or 226*
>
> *(2) 270 days after such request.*

[*11 U.S.C. §1231 (new text in italics)*]

In summary, Code section 346 is modified to provide the following, related to IRC sections 1398 and 1399:

- If section 1398 of the Internal Revenue Code of 1986 provides that a separate taxable estate or entity is created upon the filing of a bankruptcy case a separate taxable estate is also created for state and local tax purposes. Under IRC section 1398 a separate estate is created for an individual in chapters 7 and 11. If the case is dismissed, the estate would not file separate returns for state and local tax purposes as is true for federal tax purposes. All income and expenses related to the estate would be reported on the individual's return for both federal and state and local tax purposes. The trustee or debtor-in-possession has the duty to make tax returns that are required under applicable state and local law.
- If section 1399 of the Internal Revenue Code of 1986 provides that no separate taxable entity is created upon the filing of a bankruptcy case for federal tax purposes as would be the case if the entity filing the petition is not an individual, no separate taxable estate is created for state and local purposes as well. Thus, the trustee has the duty to make required corporate and partnership income tax returns. Such returns would be filed in the normal manner, as if a bankruptcy petition was not filed. The estate is liable for any tax imposed on such corporation or partnership, but not for any tax imposed on partners or members. Partnership taxable income is generally passed through and taxed to the partner or member of such partnership. This income received by an individual from a partnership, regardless of whether the partnership is in bankruptcy or not, would be reported as income on the return filed by the individual's bankruptcy estate.
- The bankruptcy estate is required to use the same accounting method used by the debtor immediately before the commencement of the case, provided such method is appropriate for state and local tax purposes.
- The time and manner of filing state and local income tax returns shall be determined under applicable nonbankrutpcy law.
- State and local income tax returns must be filed in all chapter 7 cases even though there may not be net taxable income over the pendency of a chapter 7 case. Prior to the 2005 Act as noted above, no returns were required if there was no taxable income over the pendency of the chapter 7 case. Thus, minimum franchise tax and income tax provisions imposed by many state governments may now apply universally to taxpayers in chapter 7 bankruptcy.
- In the year in which the bankruptcy petition is filed, the debtor's tax period will terminate only if and to the extent

that the taxable period of such debtor terminates under IRC section 1398. Thus, the election to end the taxable year the day before the petition is filed will apply to state and local taxes only if the election is made to file a short taxable year return for federal tax purposes.

- Transfers of property from the debtor to the estate or from the estate to the debtor are not treated as a disposition for state and local income tax purposes, except to the extent that such transfer is treated as a disposition under the Internal Revenue Code of 1986. Thus, abandonment of property that is not considered a sale for federal tax purposes will not be a sale for state and local tax purposes.
- State and local income tax is imposed at rates generally applicable to the same types of entities. In other words, for example, bankruptcy estates of individuals will be taxed at rates generally applicable to individuals and corporate estates will be taxed at corporate tax rates.
- The trustee is required to withhold and make appropriate payments of state and local taxes on payment of claims for wages, salaries, commission, dividends, interest, or other payments. Such payment has the same priority as the underlying claim and is to be made at a time and in a manner required by such tax law.
- For state and local income tax purposes, in a Title 11 case for which a new tax entity is created, this entity shall succeed to all tax attributes available to be carried over from one taxable period to a subsequent taxable period. To the extent such tax attributes still exist at the time the case is closed, they revert back to the debtor. The estate may carry back any loss or tax attribute to a prepetition tax period of the debtor if the applicable state or local law provides for a carryback and the same or a similar tax attribute may be carried back by the estate to such a taxable period of the debtor under the Internal Revenue Code of 1986.

(c) Impact of Changes

Since 1960, many significant differences have existed between federal income tax provisions and state and local income tax provisions when bankruptcy is involved. In the 2005 Act, section 719 attempts to reconcile many of these discrepancies by requiring that state and local law follow the existing federal rules that are now applicable to bankruptcy estates. The impact of these changes, however, may be limited because, while the differences existed, many tax professionals and debtors used the federal tax basis for state and local tax purposes.

There will, however, be more state and local income tax returns filed in chapter 7 cases and minimum tax amounts will be paid because the provisions that returns need only be filed for state and local tax purposes if income was earned during the entire bankruptcy proceeding has been repealed. As noted above, minimum franchise tax and income tax provisions imposed by many state governments may now apply universally to taxpayers in chapter 7 bankruptcy.

15.3 Cancellation of Indebtedness and Preserving Net Operating Losses (2005 Act Section 719)

(a) Practice Prior to 2005 Act

Cancellation of Indebtedness

Code section 346(j)(1) provided that, for state and local tax purposes, gain from debt forgiveness or discharge was not recognized by the estate, debtor, or successor to the debtor; however, tax attributes were reduced. Code section 346(j) provided that only two attributes were reduced for state and local tax purposes:

- Net operating loss carryover
- Basis of debtor's property but not in excess of the liabilities immediately after discharge.

Code section 346(j)(3) indicated that net operating loss (NOL) carryover is the first attribute to be reduced, but did not indicate the time at which the deduction should be made. It was presumed that the deduction would be made at the time of the discharge or forgiveness resulting that none of net operating losses for the year in which the discharge occurs would be reduced unless (1) there was closing of the books as of the day the petition was filed, or (2) the taxpayer interpreted this section to mean that the total net operating losses for the year be prorated, based on time, between those losses incurred prior to the filing of the petition and those incurred after the filing of the petition. For federal tax purposes, the deductions take place after the computation of the tax loss for the year in which the discharge occurs. As a result of this timing difference, the tax impact of a discharge for state and federal purposes may differ significantly, due to the fact that net operating loss is often very large in the year the petition is filed.

The only other tax attribute that must be reduced is basis in property. No distinction was made between depreciable or nondepreciable property. Also, because no timing difference was provided in Code section 346, it could have presumed that the basis would be reduced as of the date the discharge occurs. For federal tax purposes, it takes place as of the first day of the taxable year after the year in which the discharge occurs.

The debtor could have elected to include the gain from the discharge of debt in income, rather than reduce the basis of property under Code section 346(j)(6). For example, a chapter 11 debtor in a very low bracket for state income tax purposes may prefer to report the income and then be able to deduct depreciation expenses in future years when a higher tax bracket would apply. Code section 346(j)(6) did not indicate the order in which basis would be reduced. There was no provision for the debtor to elect to first reduce depreciable property and then reduce tax attributes; however, there is such a provision for federal tax purposes.

Stock for Debt

Section 346(j)(7) provided that no income from debt forgiveness or discharge was recognized when an equity security was issued in satisfaction of its debt. Since the passage of the Bankruptcy Tax Act of 1980, several restrictions have been placed on the exchange of stock for debt. It appears that most of these restrictions did not apply for state and local tax purposes.

Net Operating Loss Carryback and Carryover

The extent to which the Bankruptcy Code will apply to a carryback or carryover of tax attributes in a reorganization was questionable. If the Bankruptcy Code was silent on a tax issue, it was generally presumed that the state and local tax laws should have applied.

Many states and local taxing authorities have tax laws that conform to the provisions of the Internal Revenue Code. State and local conformity can mean complete conformity or just the use of federal taxable income as the starting point for the determination of the state or local tax liability. Other states and local taxing authorities have their own laws that specify how tax liability is to be determined.

With the increase in the number of very large bankruptcies involving many legal entities, the problems associated with state and local taxes increased. Often, a plan provides for the reduction of the number of entities, but, for federal tax purposes, the reduction alone did not prevent the net operating losses from surviving. However, for state and local tax purposes the survival of the net operating losses was certain. Careful planning was therefore needed to preserve as much of the net operating loss as possible.

If the state and local tax laws followed the federal tax attribute carryover under IRC section 381, the net operating losses may have survived. Some states and localities adopted the federal law with added restrictions. One such restriction might be that, in order to carry forward the net operating losses in a reorganization from a subsidiary that was merged into the surviving entity, the subsidiary must have been subject to state and local taxes in the period from which the loss arose.

Some states, while not directly incorporating the provisions of IRC section 381, indirectly provided for the adoption of the federal laws by using the federal taxable income, after net operating losses, as the starting point for determining state and local taxable income.[1] Some states allowed carryforwards but not carrybacks, and some states also limited the time period for carryforwards to a period of less than 20 years or even less than 15 years. Some states also limited the use of net operating losses where the entity was not subject to a state or local tax in the year when the loss occurred.

(b) Changes Enacted

Cancellation of Indebtedness

Section 346(j) as noted above was revised to provide:

> *(j)* (1) *For purposes of any State or local law imposing a tax on or measured by income,* income is not realized by the estate, the debtor, or a successor to the debtor by reason of discharge of indebtedness, *if any, that such income is subject to tax under the Internal Revenue Code of 1986.*
>
> *(2) Whenever the Internal Revenue Code of 1986 provides that the amount excluded from gross income in respect of the discharge of indebtedness in a case under this title shall be applied to reduce the tax attributes of the debtor or the estate, a similar reduction shall be made under any State or local law imposing a tax on or measured by income to the extent such State or local law recognizes such attributes. Such State or local law may also provide for the reduction of other attributes to the extent that the full amount of income from the discharge of indebtedness has not been applied.*

[*11 U.S.C. §346(j) (new text in italics)*]

In summary section 346 also provides the following, related to the cancellation of indebtedness and the reduction of tax attributes:

---

[1] O'Neill & Ruez, "State and Local Tax Issues to a Debtor in Bankruptcy," in *Bezozo & Phelan, Bankruptcy Taxation: Critical Current Issues* 532–533 (1991).

- For state and local income tax purposes, income from the cancellation of indebtedness is not realized by the estate, the debtor, or the successor to the debtor unless such income is taxable under the Internal Revenue Code, especially sections 61 and 108.
- The provisions in IRC sections 108 and 1017, requiring the reduction of tax attributes associated with nontaxable cancellation of debt income, apply for state and local income tax purposes to the extent applicable state and local law recognizes such attributes. If there are state or local laws providing for the reduction of other attributes, such reduction should be made to the extent the discharge of indebtedness has not been fully applied.

Net Operating Loss Carryback and Carryover

The modifications to Code section 346 by the 2005 Act did not address the issues of the carryover or carryback of a corporation's net operating losses.

(c) Impact of Changes

As previously discussed, the tax impact of cancellation of indebtedness was generally less for state and local tax purposes than for federal tax purposes. Most of these advantages are no longer available, such as the order of the reduction of tax attributes and the attributes to be addressed. Due to the fact that Code section 346 does not address net operating losses for corporations, the uncertainties regarding the extent to which net operating losses can be preserved for state and local tax purposes continue under the 2005 Act.

15.4 Effective Date of Changes

As with most of the changes made by the 2005 Act, these changes are effective with respect to cases commenced on or after October 17, 2005.

Chapter 16
Impact of the 2005 Act

16.1 Introduction

The balance of power between creditors and the debtor has changed significantly as a result of the Bankruptcy Abuse Prevention and Consumer Protection Act of 2005 (2005 Act). Creditors, including taxing authorities—especially for local and state taxes—for both businesses and consumers have improved their position significantly as a result of the 2005 Act.

16.2 Impact on Businesses

As a result of the 2005 Act, businesses will, among other things, need more advanced planning and more cash up-front and in the first few years after filing; they may be more likely to attempt out-of-court settlements.

(a) Filings Before October 17, 2005

First, businesses in financial difficulty that may need to seek the protection offered by filing a chapter 11 petition will find it advantageous to file before October 17, 2005. By doing so, these businesses will get a better deal on taxes, have extended time to reject leases and executory contracts, and will not be forced to file a chapter 11 plan within 18 months.

(b) More Prebankruptcy Planning

Because of the limitation on the rejection of leases and executory contracts, debtors, especially those in the retail industry, will need to complete or at least perform a significant amount of the analysis of their outstanding leases and executory contracts prior to filing.

Generally, there is a discrepancy between how those drafting the bankruptcy law see the bankruptcy process and how the process actually works, especially for the larger chapter 11s. One of the key advantages of the chapter 11 process is the debtor is granted time to solve its operational problems before it emerges from chapter 11. In many situations, it takes longer than 18 months to effectively evaluate and begin the process of implementing operational aspects of reorganizing the business. Now it will be necessary for more of this analysis to be completed prior to filing. While this process may seem helpful and certainly is encouraged, there are several benefits, including the automatic stay, that are realized by being in bankruptcy but are unavailable to debtors while the analysis is being completed.

Prebankruptcy planning may be needed to limit goods ordered within 20 days prior to filing. Because of the need to make deposits for utility services, planning will be required to see the extent to which payments for prepetition services may not be made.

(c) More Cash Needed After Filing

The 2005 Act initiated several changes that will make it more costly to file chapter 11 and at the same time significantly increase the demands on cash during the time period immediately after filing and during the years following confirmation.

The increase in cash requirements immediately after filing includes the following:

- Key employees who stay with the business once the petition has been filed will demand larger cash payments due to the 2005 Act limitations on incentive plans. Prior to the 2005 Act, certain key employees were willing to take less cash at the beginning of the case for various incentives and potential recovery on emergence from chapter 11.
- Funds needed at the time of filing are increased due to new requirements for utility deposits; such deposits were not often required prior to the 2005 Act.
- Taxes incurred in chapter 11 must now be paid as ordinary course of business transactions; prior to the 2005 Act such payments were often delayed.
- Creditors are now entitled to an administrative expense for goods shipped within 20 days prior to filing; previously such claims, unless subject to reclamation, were considered prepetition claims.
- In addition to the 20-day period, the reclamation period has been increased from 10 days to 45 days prior to filing, resulting in a larger number of goods that must be returned or granted an administrative expense status.

Changes in the time period and terms of payment for taxes will require larger cash outlays during early years following plan confirmation. The interest rate some states and local taxing authorities can demand on prepetition taxes may result in these taxes being paid over a shorter time period, thus affecting postconfirmation cash needs.

(d) More Effort to Avoid Filing

Several changes included in the 2005 Act may encourage more debtors to attempt to resolve their financial problems outside the bankruptcy process. Among these factors are the following:

- Restrictions on the ability of the debtor to retain key employees once a petition has been filed.
- Limits on the time period for assumption of commercial leases.
- Restriction of time period for debtors to file plan.
- Limitations on the ability to adjust taxes (especially state and local).

(e) Summary: Change in Strategies Prior to Filing

In summary, there will be significant changes in strategies prior to filing. Among them are the following:

- Obtain access to larger amounts of cash just prior to filing or immediately after filing. This may be in the form of larger lines of credit or special efforts to increase cash balance prior to filing.
- Complete four-wall analysis prior to filing to help determine the leases that should be rejected or assumed.
- Be more selective of time to file petition. For example, a large retail outlet would not want to file a petition so the maximum seven months extension would end during the peak business season. Debtors would want to avoid having to make a decision to assume or reject leases before sales results for each store during the peak season are known. More important, debtors would not want leases terminated at the peak of the business season.
- Complete as much work as possible toward restructuring operations and financial structure before filing. Such action allows debtors to obtain confirmation of plans before exclusivity period ends and to spread taxes over a longer time period (the five-year limit for taxes begins to run as of the petition date under the 2005 Act).
- Plan carefully for postpetition employment of management and professionals in an attempt to comply with provisions requiring such actions be justified by "the facts and circumstances of the case" under Code section 503(c)(3).
- Begin the preplanning process as early as possible and establish salaries as high as possible within the revised guidelines under Code section 503.

- Assess the cash demands for deposits with utilities and negotiate the amount and nature of such deposits required once the petition has been filed. Consider extent to which bills for prepetition services should not be paid prior to filing.
- Evaluate purchases made prior to filing to minimize amount of administrative expense claims for goods received within 20 days prior to filing and goods subject to reclamation 45 days prior to filing.

16.3 Impact on Consumers

(a) Increase in Filings Prior to October 17, 2005

Prior to the effective date of the 2005 Act, it is anticipated there will be an increase in both consumer and business filings, as previously noted. Many debtors having financial problems would be much better off filing before the 2005 Act becomes effective, for many reasons discussed throughout this publication.

(b) Use of Chapter 13

Chapter 13 will be used primarily by those that fail to satisfy the means test and must convert to chapter 13 or have their petition dismissed. The key incentive—a super discharge that encouraged debtors to file chapter 13 and pay at least part of their debts over time—was terminated in the 2005 Act. The chapter 13 time period over which payments must be made under the plan has been increased from three to five years.

(c) Cost of Filing

Due to the additional responsibilities placed on those filing bankruptcy petitions, the cost of filing is expected to increase significantly. Unfortunately, some very qualified professionals may cease to serve the needs of filers, because of the potential liability associated with filing individual chapter 7 petitions. Also, it may be more difficult for qualified individuals to file returns on a pro bono basis, requiring those that can least afford it to pay for a petition to be prepared.

(d) Reduction of Abuses

No doubt the means testing provisions will reduce some of the abuses occurring prior to the 2005 Act by requiring debtors to make payments from future income under chapter 11 or 13. Additionally some debtors who might have previously filed bankruptcy may decide not to file and either make arrangements out of court to make debt payments or continue to make debt payments without filing or seeking relief out of court. Other provisions included in the 2005 Act designed to eliminate or reduce the perceived abuses are as follow:

- Limitations on moving prior to filing to states with no cap on homestead exemptions
- Increase in time between filings during which the debtor cannot obtain a discharge
- Reduction of amount allowed for homestead exemptions to the extent homestead was obtained through fraudulent conversion of exempt assets during the 10 years prior to filing
- Increase in the number of situations where the automatic stay does not apply
- Requirement that both income earned during bankruptcy by the debtor and future income of the debtor be used to make debt payments
- Elimination of the super discharge in chapter 13
- Requirement that the debtor file tax returns
- Requirement that the debtor file documents and schedules or be subject to automatic dismissal

(e) Mandatory Credit Counseling and Educational Course

All individuals filing a bankruptcy petition must receive credit counseling from an approved nonprofit budget and credit counseling agency. Additionally, a discharge may not be granted in chapter 13 unless the debtor has completed an education course in personal financial management.

16.4 Bankruptcy Judges Become Referees Again

Years ago, the predecessors of bankruptcy judges were known as referees. However, prior to the time the Bankruptcy Reform Act of 1978 was put into effect, their title had been changed to reflect the use of judgment instead of the application of rules in the performance of their duties. The 2005 Act has now forced a large step backward by removing judgment from the equation of a considerable number of issues previously reserved for bankruptcy judges. For example, prior to the 2005 Act, a bankruptcy judge could have, on the judge's own motion or by a motion of the U.S. trustee, dismissed an abusive petition with mostly consumer debts. While the number of petitions dismissed was limited, it is important to recognize that the Code was written in favor of the debtor. For example, the Code provided that a party in interest could not make a motion to dismiss a petition and that there "shall be a presumption in favor of granting the relief requested by the debtor." Congress could have changed the Code to make it easier to dismiss chapter 11 petitions due to abuse, but at the same time still have provided a safety net for debtors with legitimate need for such relief, allowing the bankruptcy judge to effectively serve as "judge" in a court of equity. Nonetheless, Congress elected to go the other way and has established a mathematical equation applicable to all debtors with few exceptions, leaving the "bankruptcy referees" to determine whether the equation has been accurately carried out.

Other areas where the 2005 Act limits the use of judgment by bankruptcy judges include the limitation on time to extend the period to reject leases, the lack of authority to extend exclusivity period beyond 18 months, and the restrictions on allowing bankruptcy judges to determine the validity of key employee retention plans.

A

B

C

D

E

F

G

H

I

K

L

M

N

P

R

S

T

U

W

About the Organizations

The American Institute of Certified Public Accountants (AICPA). The AICPA is the national, professional organization for all certified public accountants (CPAs). Its mission is to provide members with the resources, information, and leadership that enable them to provide valuable services in the highest professional manner to benefit the public as well as employers and clients. The AICPA works with state CPA organizations and gives priority to those areas where public reliance on CPA skills is most significant. The Institute seeks to fulfill its mission by concentrating its efforts in the following areas:

- *Advocacy.* Serves as the national representative of CPAs before governments, regulatory bodies, and other organizations in protecting and promoting members' interests.
- *Certification and Licensing.* Seeks the highest possible level of uniform certification and licensing standards and promotes and protects the CPA designation.
- *Communications.* Promotes public awareness and confidence in the integrity, objectivity, competence, and professionalism of CPAs and monitors the needs and views of CPAs.
- *Recruiting and Education.* Encourages highly qualified individuals to become CPAs and supports the development of outstanding academic programs.
- *Standards and Performance.* Establishes professional standards; assists members in continually improving their professional conduct, performance, and expertise; and monitors such performance to enforce current standards and requirements.

The Association of Insolvency and Restructuring Advisors (AIRA). The AIRA is a nationwide not-for-profit organization serving the needs of business turnaround, restructuring, and bankruptcy practitioners. Membership consists of CPAs, financial advisors, attorneys, workout consultants, trustees, and others involved in insolvency and bankruptcy practice. In 1992, AIRA established the Certified Insolvency and Restructuring Advisor (CIRA) program to recognize professionals who have demonstrated a high level of competency through completion of a course of study, examination, and comprehensive experience requirements. AIRA recently also established the Certification in Distressed Business Valuation (CDBV) program to train and accredit professionals in the valuation of distressed assets, including distressed and/or bankrupt companies. Through a variety of membership programs and conferences, AIRA endeavors to provide the highest quality of services to its members to help them serve their clients.